GETTING ORGANIZED!

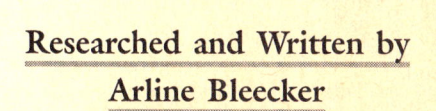

Researched and Written by
Arline Bleecker

Contents

H **HINTS IN THE KITCHEN:** How to eliminate 200 lbs. of kitchen grease a year, splatterproof with a window shade, make turkey basting easy, add a mini-pantry, etc.................................**7**

O **OVERCOME THE PAPER JAM:** End the paper push, start a foolproof filing system, get your hands on any piece of paper in a jiffy, keep track of insurance claims, etc....................**17**

W **WHERE TO STORE WHATNOTS:** From where in a teeny apartment to place a full-sized ladder to making good use of that space on your garage ceiling..**24**

T **TRICKS FOR PHONE EFFICIENCY:** How to screen calls, get the most from your answering machine, avoid interruptions, have phone time for yourself and teach kids to take messages. **30**

O **OTHER ROOMS TO ORGANIZE:** Store linens, books and clothing, what to keep or throw away, turn a window shade into a chalkboard, keep your jewelry tangle free, etc............................**33**

G **GET A HANDLE ON YOUR TOOLS:** What ELSE a record album jacket can store, how to guarantee your neighbor returns your tools and a solution for stray screwdrivers.........................**42**

E **EKE OUT MORE MINUTES:** Ideas to stretch your day, cure lateness, unravel holiday lights in a flash, speed nail polish drying and endure that wait in the doctor's office. **45**

T **TRIM YOUR LEGWORK:** From the amazing versatility of plastic bags and the value of out-of-town phone books to shortcuts for emptying wastebaskets, etc...**51**

O OTHERS CAN HELP: How to "volunteer" your kids, spouse, partner and roommate. **55**

R REMEMBER THE SMALL THINGS: From feeding the parking meter and changing smoke alarm batteries to rehanging wall arrangements...why a tape recorder is a terrific repairman, etc...**63**

G GARDENING GOODIES: Bushed gardeners get a lift from planting seeds without bending, making a garden shed from a mailbox, watering without effort, and much more. **68**

A ACCESS IS EVERYTHING: Code your stockings so you always pick the good ones, never again misplace a matching belt, balance a recipe so it stands straight up, and more...................**70**

N NOVEL WAYS TO CUT CLUTTER: Stockpile spices in a shoe bag, store vegetables in an old nylon stocking, whip up rubber bands from a rubber glove, and more. **75**

I INNOVATIONS FOR ENTERTAINING: Rig a makeshift coat room, turn a household appliance into a salad spinner, whip cream ahead of time and plan for perfect parties, etc................**78**

Z ZIP THROUGH CHORES: Switch errands with your neighbors, clean mini-blinds in half the time, beat the waiting room wait, shortcuts for making your bed, and more............................**80**

E EFFICIENCY CAN SAVE YOU MONEY: Stay under your credit limit, what your insurance company should know about your safe-deposit box, make a new broom last longer, and more........**85**

D DETAILS, DETAILS, DETAILS: Preview a permanent wave, protect raw eggs on a camping trip, take the guesswork out of cleaning wallpaper, select a suitable family pet, etc............................**90**

 ...AND THEN SOME: Set small goals and take time out to avoid getting OVERorganized, reduce visual clutter, a formula for getting enough sleep, and more. **95**

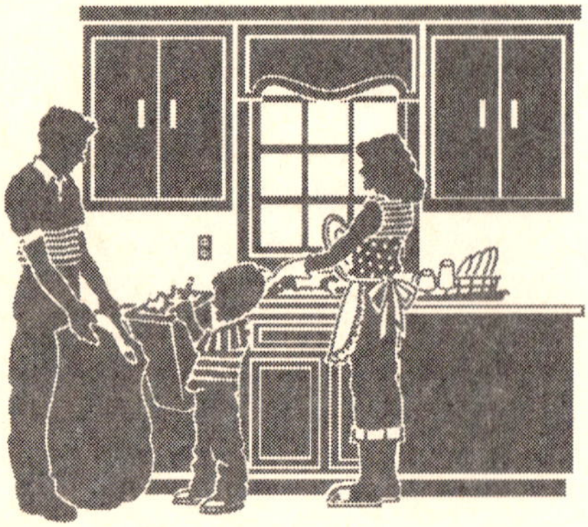

Hints in the Kitchen

✔ **Temporary work space:** Mount a flip-up shelf on a wall to make a temporary counter. When you're through, just fold it down and out of the way.

✔ **Work smarter:** Attach a fold-out work shelf next to the sink at stool height. It'll take the load off your feet when preparing meals.

✔ **Snack bar:** Set your flip-up or fold-out shelf at the end of a counter. It beats bringing food to the table and makes cleanup a snap for quickie meals.

✔ **Simplify grocery unpacking:** Place a flip-up hinged shelf near the fridge and set your grocery bags on it for easy reach. This can save hundreds of steps when you're unpacking groceries from the market.

✔ **Easy grocery storing:** When unpacking groceries, put all refrigerated items together next to the fridge so you open the door just once.

✔ **Pots and pans:** Store these with S-hooks on a chain hung from the ceiling in a corner.

✔ **Date spices:** Bottle fresh spices and attach labels that clearly indicate what they are as well as the date of purchase. Keep them near your cooking area, but store the excess in a cool, dark place.

✔ **Too many spices:** Alphabetize spice jars to find them in a hurry.

✔ **Spice space:** Slip a shelf expander into or under your existing spice cabinet. Its step-like shape lets you arrange jars like sports fans in a bleacher. (This is also great for your medicine cabinet.)

✔ **Lazy Susan:** Store spice jars on one of these at the front of a cabinet or, if you've got the counter space, out in full view.

✔ **Mini mini-holder:** Group together those skinny packets of powdered salad dressings or soft-drink mixes in a plastic cherry tomato or strawberry box.

✔ **Save counter space:** Use spacesaving kitchen appliances that mount onto the wall or under the bottoms of cabinets.

✔ **Airy cabinet space:** Install a narrow but expandable wooden coat rack across the top of a window and hang your pots and pans from it.

✔ **Storing staples:** Keep milk, cheese, juices, etc. in the same place in your fridge so you won't waste time looking for them. Do the same for pantry staples.

✔ **Cook in volume:** Double all your recipes and freeze half for another time.

✔ **Extra soup:** Freeze leftover soup in ice cube trays and use for quick meals or for adding to gravies.

✔ *Freeze for ease:* Peel, quarter and freeze onions in a single layer in a pan. When frozen, repack in freezer bags or containers and use portions as needed.

✔ *Quick meals:* Stock up on non-perishables like canned tuna or tomato sauce and never be caught short for a last-minute meal.

✔ *One-dish meals:* Make protein-based soups, pasta salads and stews. Meals that provide all the protein, starch and vegetables in one pot are great time savers.

✔ *Smooth gravy:* Keep a pantry jar filled with equal parts flour and cornstarch. Whenever you make gravy, just mix 3 Tbs of this mixture with water in another jar, shake, and in seconds, you'll have a ready-to-add gravy paste.

✔ *Utensils:* Save time by presorting forks, knives and spoons as you load them into your dishwasher's utensil compartment.

✔ *Measuring ingredients:* Do it by weight instead of by measuring cup. Place a bowl on a 2-lb. scale and jot down the weight of each ingredient. Then, whenever you make that dish, just use the one bowl and scale.

✔ *Quicker cooking:* Use wide, flat cooking pots and casserole dishes to speed up cooking time.

✔ *Speed heating #1:* Let food stand at room temperature before reheating to shorten cooking time.

✔ *Speed heating #2:* Cut up smaller-sized pieces of vegetables or chicken, serve thinner cuts of beef or pork, or substitute lamb chops for leg of lamb.

✔ *Turkey basting:* Drape a few strips of bacon over your roasting turkey to baste it automatically.

✔ **Whipping whites:** Let egg whites stand at room temperature before beating. They'll fluff up faster.

✔ **Vent oven exhaust:** Install one on your stove. It eliminates as much as 200 lbs. of grease buildup a year.

✔ **Muffin tins:** Line them with cupcake papers to save cleanup time.

✔ **Serving tray:** Hang one from a hook on a wall or on the side of a cabinet. Once it's there, you'll be amazed how often you use it.

✔ **Locate strategically:** Store things together that you usually use together. Glasses, for example, are handiest if placed right near the sink; pots, pans and covers should be near the stove.

✔ **Pot covers:** Store lids together in one place. Stand them on their sides in descending size order in a cabinet, get a pot lid organizer from a housewares store, or just designate a deep kitchen drawer for this purpose.

✔ **Flat items:** Store pizza pans, cookie sheets or cooling racks vertically. Use either a pot-lid organizer or one of those desk organizers designed to hold file folders upright.

✔ **Speedy breakfasts:** Store breakfast items together so you can reach for them in a jiffy, no matter how bleary-eyed you are in the morning.

✔ **Gadgetize:** Use time – and labor – saving devices like an electric carving knife and a food processor. Even gadgets that are cumbersome to clean – like a garlic press – will save you time. Look for those with self-cleaning features.

✔ *Countertop appliances:* Store all your most useful appliances in sight at all times so they're always available – even if it means getting socket extenders to accommodate your electric appliances.

✔ *Trash bins:* Drill a pair of holes near the top of an inexpensive plastic wastebasket, then hang it from cup hooks on the inside of the cabinet door under the sink.

✔ *Recycling bins:* Install slide-out double trash bins inside an under-sink cabinet. By using one for trash and the other for recyclables, you presort as you go.

✔ *Double-duty bowls:* Buy a serving bowl or casserole dish that's also oven/freezer safe and attractive enough to bring to the table.

✔ *Oven cleanup:* Keep a canister of salt alongside the oven for cleaning up spills. Just sprinkle on the spill immediately. When the oven cools, brush away burnt-on food with a damp sponge.

✔ *Prevent refrigerator mildew:* Wipe down your refrigerator occasionally with white vinegar. It'll prevent a bigger problem later on.

✔ *Leftovers:* Experiment with exotic uses for leftovers. Today's turkey can be tomorrow's turkey tetrazzini and almost any leftover can be turned into soup.

✔ *Reduce splatter:* When you are frying foods, invert a metal colander over the frying pan to prevent hard-to-clean oil splatters.

✔ *Splatterproofing:* Install a sheet of plastic on the wall above the stove for easy cleanup. Or hang a washable window shade upside down. When you cook, pull up the shade and attach to a mounted cup hook.

✔ *Prevent sticking:* Heat the frying pan before adding oil or butter. It's guaranteed to keep food from sticking.

✔ *Clogs:* Pour ½ cup washing soda (not baking soda) directly down the drain, then slowly add 2 qts. hot water. This weekly preventive maintenance will ensure that clogs will never be a problem.

✔ *Loose salt:* Tightly wrap a piece of aluminum foil around the salt shaker or add a couple of dozen grains of rice. This method keeps salt pourable by keeping dampness out.

✔ *Eliminate scavenger hunts:* If your supermarket receipt clearly lists every item you purchased by name, post it on the fridge. It lets everyone know what you've bought so they can search the fridge or pantry for their snacks.

✔ *Convenient utensils:* Put a Lazy Susan or wide-mouthed bowl or basket next to the stove so every utensil is within reach.

✔ *Shelf storage:* For under-sink storage, install wire sliding shelves on the sides of the cabinet. Be careful not to obstruct pipes.

✔ *Wall grid systems:* Use these to hang everything from paper towels and measuring cups to pots and utensils – all in full view for quick access.

✔ *Kitchen office:* If your house has no room for an office, use the kitchen table as a desk. Designate one kitchen drawer for all the supplies you'll need, like stamps, envelopes and pencils.

✔ *Trivet trivia:* Nail or staple a stiff accordion-pleated paper file folder to the inside of a cabinet door. It's just the right size – for holding lids, trivets and other flat kitchen objects.

✔ *Food wraps:* Store plastic wrap, aluminum foil and garbage bags upright in one of those practical wrap-and-bag organizers that hangs inside a cabinet door. Or slip them into the slots of a wine rack.

✔ *Plastic wrap:* Keep it in the fridge. The cold will prevent the plastic from sticking.

✔ *Knife rack:* Mount a magnetized knife rack on the wall. This simple technique lets you see the whole knife at a glance.

✔ *Mini-pantry:* Add shelves to a narrow cabinet that once held an old-fashioned fold-out ironing board. It's ideal as a mini-pantry for cans and spices.

✔ *From broom to room:* Fill a broom closet with shelves to create a pantry (or a linen closet) that holds lots more than an unshelved closet. Hang your brooms on the back of a door.

✔ *Open storage:* Paint a picture of a tree on one wall and use cup hooks along the branches to hang pots and pans. It lends an artistic touch and saves space.

✔ *String dispenser:* Mount a plastic berry basket on the wall, pop in a ball of cooking string with the lead end slipped through an opening in the basket and you have a handy dispenser for tying up that Sunday roast.

✔ *Recipe clippings:* Store recipes you find in newspapers and magazines in a big envelope taped to the inside cover of your cookbook.

✔ *Coupon keeping:* Pack current coupons inside a letter-sized envelope, then use the back of the envelope for writing your shopping list. Check off those items you already have coupons for and you'll never forget to use them at checkout.

✔ *Coupon organizing:* Arrange coupons by expiration date and circle or highlight the date for easy spotting. If you have a bunch, make a file. Separate first by month, then by product type. At the end of the month, throw out expired ones.

✔ *Unclutter the fridge:* Throw out any suspicious-looking food in your fridge or freezer.

✔ *Savvy freezing:* Keep track of how long your frozen foods are storable by posting a freezer-storage guide inside your pantry cabinet. Label everything you freeze and include a "throw-out" date.

✔ *Prevent fridge fritz:* Stick a meat thermometer into a carton of ice cream to check freezer temperature. It should read 0 to 6 degrees F. The same thermometer in a glass of water should read 35 to 40 degrees in the fridge.

✔ *Supplies:* Stash your organizing tools – like marking pens, twist ties and labels for identifying and dating food – in a flatware divider.

✔ *Lunch station:* In a breadbox, store all the non-perishable things you use to prepare the kids' school lunches – sandwich bags, twist ties, bread, cookies, even spare change for treats. Keep lunch boxes in a nearby drawer.

✔ *Minimize cleanup:* While cooking, return used ingredients immediately where they belong and toss all wrappers and scraps. This saves time and keeps you from forgetting whether or not you added that pinch of baking soda.

✔ *Grate cleaner:* Clean kitchen graters with a toothbrush.

✔ *Magnetized memo pads:* Stick a magnetized memo pad on your fridge. It's perfect for last-minute shopping lists because you can just rip off the top sheet and take it with you when you go.

✔ *Built-ins are better:* Invest in built-in kitchen appliances. They have less surface area to get dirty in the first place.

✔ *Project planning:* Target only one project at a time. If today's goal is to alphabetize your spice collection, don't also try to clean out the fridge.

✔ *Recipe-ready:* Before you use a recipe, read it completely. Assemble each ingredient as you read so you won't have to scramble at the last minute. Take out all the pots, pans and serving dishes, too.

✔ *Prepare for accidents:* Place a towel in the bottom of the kitchen sink in order to spare yourself the heartbreak of glassbreak. It will cushion fine china or crystal when you wash them.

✔ *Cleaning carry-all:* To make cleaning day easier, stash your household cleaning basics – like cleansers, paper towels and sponges – in a plastic bucket. That way, you won't have to run back and forth for what you need.

✔ *Paper bags:* Stack your brown paper grocery bags neatly in a magazine rack.

✔ *Orderly junk:* Instead of plowing through those tiny odds and ends piling up in your junk drawer, arrange them in ice cube trays or in those big plastic covers from cans of aerosol deodorant.

✔ *Rarely used utensils:* Get a handle on your infrequently used utensils (or those that are so small they keep disappearing in the drawer). Store them in the compartments of a see-through shoe bag that hangs behind the pantry door.

✔ *Timer reminder:* When you put food onto the stove or into the oven, set a timer to ring five minutes before the food is done. This eliminates that dash to make a sauce or gives you time to take care of any other last-minute preparations.

✔ *Test cookies:* Before baking batches of cookies, test-bake just one. That way, you'll know if you need to adjust the recipe, timing or oven temperature. This test could actually save you time – as well as the disappointment of cookie failure!

✔ *Chop cleanup time:* For stirring soups, stews and just about anything you cook, use long, thick chopsticks instead of wooden spoons. They're a breeze to clean.

✔ *Block boilover:* Add a pat of butter or a few teaspoons of cooking oil to the water to keep your rice or pasta from boiling over while you are busy elsewhere.

✔ *Extra eggs:* If you have more than you'll use in the near-term, crack them open and place individually in an ice cube tray. When they're completely frozen, unmold and keep in a sealed freezer bag for future use.

16

Overcome the Paper Jam
Keeping Records

✉ **Paper pushing:** Do one of only four things with a sheet of paper:
- Act on it
- File it
- Toss it out
- Refer it to someone else

✉ **Minimize paper handling:** If you need to touch any piece of paper more than once, jot on it where it eventually should be filed and keep all such papers in a box marked "to be filed."

✉ **Mail management:** As soon as you get your mail, read it and sort it into one of these categories: "pay," "answer," "file" and "dump." Then do it!

✉ **Unpile your files:** To conveniently get your hands on important papers, use hanging folders in file drawers and vertical files on your desktop. Vertical files are also great for sorting mail.

✉ **Purge your files:** Jot down the date you receive prescriptions, perishables, restaurant and shopping guides, plus anything that includes dated materials, such as newspapers. Sort and toss on a regular basis.

✉ **Track events:** Place announcements for shows, sales and other upcoming events in one folder. On your calendar, jot down those you'd like to attend. Add a "see folder" notation to remind you to check the announcement for details. Purge monthly.

✉ *Monthly management:* Starting with the current month, make a folder for each month. In the appropriate folder, keep all those loose ends you need to remember: people to call, gifts to buy, letters to write, etc.

✉ *Files you need:* Automobile, bank, bills to pay, bills paid, correspondence, deeds and certificates, education, finances, insurance, legal documents, medical, rent/mortgage, taxes, telephone and utilities.

✉ *Personal files:* You can organize your personal life with an alphabetical filing system, too. Some common categories: auto maintenance, gift ideas, pet care, restaurants, resume, vacations, etc.

✉ *Two files:* Set up temporary files labeled "To be filed" and "To be tossed." In the first, put items that need to be permanently saved. In the second, put dated material. Each month, file the first and dump the second.

✉ *The instruction riddle:* Set up a folder just to hold those special instructions, like how to program the VCR, how to clean the wicker sofa, etc.

✉ *Warranties and manuals:* For troubleshooting and record-keeping, keep these in an expanding file folder. Label the sections: dishwasher, furnace/water heater, furniture, home entertainment, microwave, outdoor equipment, small appliances, stove/fridge, tools, vacuum, washer/dryer and miscellaneous.

✉ **Serial numbers:** File serial numbers and receipts with your warranties and manuals. If the item is tax deductible, photocopy the receipt and keep it in your tax file.

✉ **Medical records:** Keep a complete record of immunizations, hospitalizations, surgeries and diseases. Make a separate file for each family member or use a loose-leaf binder with a page for each person. Do the same for all your pets.

✉ **Doctor's visits:** Make a list of symptoms and questions to ask before calling or visiting your doctor. Take a pad and pen to the doctor's office to jot down last-minute questions. Take notes when the doctor explains the diagnosis and treatment. File it in your medical folder.

✉ **Insurance claims:** In a folder, keep a sample claim form with your insurance number, filing instructions and blank forms. Staple a ledger page to the folder to jot down claims and bills, doctor's name, procedure and date, date of claim and date of payment. A blank in the payment column shows your claim is pending.

✉ **Preprep postage:** Have a rubber stamp made with your name and address. Set out 100 envelopes and a roll of 100 stamps. While you're watching TV, put one stamp and your return address on each envelope.

✉ **Postage supplies:** For heavier mail, keep a supply of assorted-sized blank envelopes and extra stamps handy.

✉ **Flag important items:** Post a sheet of sticky yellow notepad paper on anything that has something important in it and briefly scrawl on it whatever action you want to take.

✉ **Highlighter pens:** Use them for flagging things you want to reread. In books or magazines, they'll speed your search for the information. Use it in your calendar book, too!

📧 *Date all payments:* When you pay a bill, immediately date it and mark it "paid," noting the check number and date. Move the bill from your bills-to-pay file into your monthly paid-bills file or, if appropriate, to your tax file.

📧 *Curtail credit cards:* If you use credit cards, use as few as possible. Fewer bills to pay and fewer stamps to lick means more time – and money – saved.

📧 *Reduce receipt runaround:* Always put your credit card receipts in the same place – either in an envelope, a file or a drawer. Keep all the month's receipts together until the bill arrives.

📧 *Customer-copy:* Get into the habit of checking that every credit card receipt you sign is legible before stuffing it into your wallet so there's no mystery to unravel at bill-paying time.

📧 *Hassle-free payments:* Pay your bills on the same day each month – just leave the envelopes unsealed. On each envelope's flap, write the bill's due date and keep them in ready-to-mail order. When it's time to send, seal and mail it.

📧 *Check-writing schedule:* Regardless of when your bills arrive, make payments no more than two separate times each month: the 1st and the 15th, or the 15th and the 30th.

📧 *Spot checks:* Designate one spot in your house for keeping all bills that have to be paid. And don't deviate from it.

📧 *Ticklers for taxes:* As you make a major deductible purchase or expenditure during the year, just drop a note into your tax file as a reminder to report it.

📧 *Managing deductibles:* If it's too much trouble to photocopy your receipts, just remember never to file one for a tax deductible item – until you've entered the amount in your tax records.

✉ **_Bank statements:_** Since the checks you write also double as receipts, be sure to put them in numerical order as soon as you get your monthly statement.

✉ **_Find checks fast:_** To quickly get your hands on any canceled check, keep an entire year's checks filed (in order) in a small box designated for that purpose. Keep the appropriate year's check transaction register in the same box.

✉ **_Junk mail:_** Get off junk mailing lists by cutting your name and address label off the package and send it back in the no-postage-necessary envelope that came with the junk! Include a note asking to please be removed from the list.

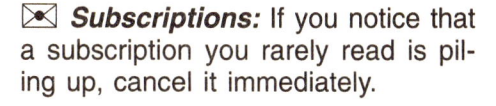

✉ **_Subscriptions:_** If you notice that a subscription you rarely read is piling up, cancel it immediately.

✉ **_Catalogue catalogs:_** Keep catalogs separate from your regular magazines and keep only the most current ones. Try categorizing them for quick retrieval.

✉ **_Coupons:_** If you find yourself with a zillion coupons you never redeem, simply stifle the urge to keep clipping.

✉ **_Sidestep misfiling:_** Use staples instead of paper clips to keep papers attached. Clips not only take up added space in your files, but they're likely to clip other things along with them and leave you with the misery of misfiling.

✉ **_Calendar cleverness:_** Right before a new year begins, transfer into your new calendar all recurring due dates and events (like tax payments, license renewals, birthdays). Use bright ink so that next year, when you need to do it again, the entries will be a snap to find.

✉ *Calendar coding:* At the front of your calendar book, keep a list of every occasion you want to remember. Code with a number, then enter just the number on the appropriate date in your calendar. Check the list to decode. This takes up less space and gives you more room to write. At year end, transfer the whole list to next year's calendar.

✉ *Household inventory:* Make a list of every item you've purchased, including purchase price, serial number and replacement cost. Store one copy in your safe deposit box and one in your freezer.

✉ *Videotape inventory:* Videotape all household items and valuables. As you shoot, describe the make, model, serial number and anything else you can think of. If you don't have video equipment, take photos and describe the details into a cassette recorder. Store the tape and photos together.

✉ *Where's what?* Start keeping a storage journal in a looseleaf notebook. Jot down where you've stashed everything.

✉ *Mini-phone list:* Copy your most frequently used phone numbers into a phone book that's small enough to carry around with you. That way, you won't have to take along your whole phone book whenever you're away from home.

✉ *Phone numbers:* To keep phone numbers at your fingertips, use one of those circular desktop card filers (Rolodex) that lets you put each name and number on a separate card arranged alphabetically.

✉ *Extra phone cards:* If you keep phone numbers on a system that uses individual file cards, keep an extra batch of blank cards behind the "Z" so you can find one quickly.

✉ **Phone list:** Organize – by category – the phone numbers of people whose services you use only on an irregular basis. Put your plumber under "P" and the electrician under "E," so you don't risk forgetting their names. You might want to cross-reference by name also.

✉ **Business cards:** Don't immediately put new numbers from business cards on your permanent phone list. Mark the date and store it temporarily in a box marked "business cards." If you haven't referred to it in a year, toss it.

✉ **Computer phone lists:** If you own a computer, use it as an electronic telephone directory. Many software programs let you enter information randomly but can retrieve it for you instantly – without you having to hunt for it.

✉ **Pencil it in:** If you use an address book, make the entries in pencil or erasable ink. It'll save having to redo them whenever someone's number or address changes.

✉ **Reading readiness:** Keep magazines and newspapers (along with your tools for reading) in a basket that you can easily carry from room to room. When you get some sit-down time, just bring the basket along.

✉ **Reader list:** List every family member's name on a piece of notepaper and staple it to the cover. Keep the magazine or paper until everyone has checked off his or her name. That way no one will miss a turn.

✉ **Handy travel kit:** For traveling, one small notebook does triple duty as a calendar, a journal and for writing notes. Staple a half-pocket in the back to keep stamps, receipts and postcards handy.

✉ **Lighten that guidebook:** Since guidebooks are updated annually, don't be timid about marking them up. Underline or circle anything that's important. Then take along only those pages you need.

Where to Store Whatnots

✤ **Bridge table:** Glue a pretty poster to the top of the table, add a protective coat of varnish, then store it in plain sight as a wall hanging.

✤ **Foul-weather gear:** On a spare wall in your utility room, install a shoe rack for hanging outdoor shoes and boots, a 6-ft. shelf and rod for adult raincoats and umbrellas, a waist-high shelf with hooks for the kids' jackets, gloves and mufflers and a plastic floor mat.

✤ **Window seat:** Install a lift-up lid for storing pillows, quilts and blankets. If there's enough wall space, add a closet on either side of the window seat as a private reading nook.

✤ **Bottles:** Cut a 6-in. diameter PVC piping into 14-in. lengths, stack side-by-side in a box and you've got an ideal storage rack for wine, sodas and more.

✤ **Long-term clothing storage:** To avoid wrinkles, remove the stored clothing every few months, refold, then store them again.

✤ **Prevent wrinkles:** Close all zippers and buttons before storing any garment.

✤ **Stain-free storage:** Clean your clothes before you store them to prevent that irreversible discoloration that somehow magically appears the following season.

✤ *Humidity-free storage:* Use corrugated boxes as inexpensive storage containers for off-season clothing. Make them humidity-resistant by spraying them with shellac.

✤ *Protect clothing:* Don't store clothing on wooden hangers. Over time, the acid in the wood can react with the fabric. Wire hangers aren't much better. Pad all non-plastic hangers with unbleached muslin or cotton.

✤ *Conserve storage space:* When you are storing clothing short term, hang several blouses or shirts of one color on a single hanger. This is not recommended for long-term storage, however.

✤ *Ladder:* Turn it into a planter and put it in a corner in plain sight. Decorate the steps with houseplants until you need it again.

✤ *Table extension leaf:* Hang it on the closet wall behind your clothes. It doesn't take up room, it's out of sight and protected from scratches.

✤ *Valuables:* Coat the inside of a jar with leftover paint. Drain and let the jar dry to an opaque finish. Use it to stash valuables.

✤ *Emergency cash:* Hide it in a pet-food box on a high shelf. Just make sure no one throws it out!

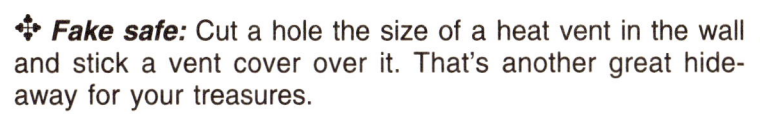

✤ *Fake safe:* Cut a hole the size of a heat vent in the wall and stick a vent cover over it. That's another great hideaway for your treasures.

✤ *Finding space:* For extra storage room, use the space below your stairs (if the stairs are enclosed). Install a door for access.

✤ **Stairs again:** To maximize the under-the-stairs space, build triangular shelf units on casters that can easily slip into the corners.

✤ **Storage bin:** Hinge a back-door step or the top step of your basement stairs so it can be raised. It's great for hiding odds and ends.

✤ **Behind the wall:** Cut out several vertical feet of space in a wall between two studs. Slip in shelves and hinge a wall hanging over it to hide the storage space. Use for china and crystal.

✤ **Add a pantry:** Convert the area between wall studs into a pantry or cabinet. Just be sure to use an inside wall!

✤ **Ceiling space:** Suspend a cabinet from your garage ceiling for extra storage space.

✤ **More shelving:** Hang under-shelf storage baskets in the linen closet. The wire shelf, available in most hardware stores, slides onto the shelf above – great for storing soap or washcloths.

✤ **Small extension cords:** Use the cardboard center from a paper towel roll to hold small extension cords.

✤ **Extension cords:** Cut two horizontal slits in a gallon plastic jug, one near the top, the other near the bottom. Make them a bit narrower than the cord. Slip one end of the cord in one slit and wind the cord around the jug. When wound, slip the other end into the second slot. Hang by handle when not in use.

✤ **Tiny paint brushes:** Slip them into drinking straws to protect them.

✤ **Charcoal:** Store briquettes in a small plastic trash can and close the lid tightly to keep out any moisture. Paint the lid black or label it to remind you that it's for charcoal only.

✥ **Keys:** Remove the spine from an old three-ring loose-leaf notebook to hold those extra keys.

✥ **Pet food:** Remove dry pet food from its bag and store in a lidded plastic trash can (new, of course!) It's neater, it stays fresh longer – and keeps pests out.

✥ **Fishing reel:** Store inside an old sweat sock for super protection.

✥ **Ornaments:** Store small Christmas balls in egg cartons and larger ornaments in the compartments of a wine-bottle carton. Sweat socks can protect those extra-large balls. Loosely place rubber bands between the balls to keep them apart.

✥ **Christmas lights:** Store strings of lights in those long tubes from wrapping paper rolls.

✥ **Togetherness:** Store together – or as closely together as possible – anything that requires some other part in order to operate, such as an electric griddle and the temperature control box.

✥ **Car trunk:** Store items you take with you regularly in the car trunk. In summer, for example, leave beach chairs and tennis equipment in the car instead of hauling them in and out of the garage every time you need them.

✥ **Auto registration:** Never leave your car registration in the glove compartment. It gives a car thief automatic proof of ownership! Keep it with you.

✥ *Collections:* Have a piece of glass cut to fit over the top of your kitchen table, coffee table or bureau. Display (and protect) your collection of old photos, stamps or postcards underneath.

✥ *Maps:* Round up all your maps and store them in a shoebox.

✥ *Pierced earrings:* Put pushpins on a large piece of corkboard on a bedroom or bathroom wall to hang pierced earrings. They're easy to get to, and it makes a decorative arrangement out of your jewelry.

✥ *Pegboards:* Put a pegboard on the inside of a closet door – and use it to hang dozens of items...ties, belts, purses and earrings.

✥ *Cedar closet:* Make a makeshift cedar closet with a new 50-gallon plastic trash can. Line it with an extra-large plastic trash bag. Sprinkle with cedar crystals or mothball flakes as you pack your clothing.

✥ *Empty suitcases:* Use them for storage. Label them with removable masking tape. And, of course, store smaller pieces of luggage inside the larger ones.

✥ *Coffee cans:* Store food, sewing supplies, even screws and nails in empty coffee cans (with plastic covers). Be sure to label clearly.

✥ *Empty glass jars:* Store dry foods like pasta, beans and cereal in empty glass jars on your countertops. They're also great desktop containers for paper clips and rubber bands.

✥ **Breadbox:** Convert a breadbox into a tool chest. It will hold all the small tools you need for small repairs.

✥ **Pack efficiently:** Pack "squares" rather than "rounds," and you'll cram more stuff into less storage space. Put non-square things into square boxes, fill the boxes, then pack or stack them next to each other. This tip works for suitcases as well as storage closets.

✥ **Buried-in-books?** Donate those you'll never read again to a charity, the hospital or your local library.

✥ **Gifts:** Get rid of that stash of really useless gifts in the attic. Storage space is too valuable to waste.

✥ **File, don't pile:** Put all that stuff piled out in the open into boxes and store it away. Just remember to label what's in every box.

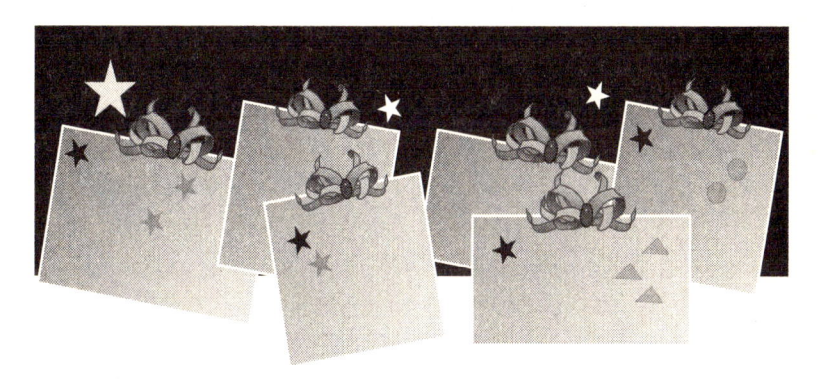

✥ **See-through boxes:** Use these to store your stuff if you're the type who has to see absolutely everything you own. They'll be gone... but not forgotten.

✥ **Be flexible:** Do whatever works for you. Put kitchen towels and soaps in a kitchen cabinet. Use the fridge for keeping nail polish or an ice bucket as a vase.

Tricks for Phone Efficiency

☎ ***Memory saves time:*** If your phone has a programmable memory, enter your most frequently dialed numbers.

☎ ***Answering machines:*** Buy an inexpensive answering machine. They're invaluable for the calls you just can't afford to miss.

☎ ***Screen calls:*** Don't let a jangling telephone decide when you should be interrupted from what you're doing. Use your answering machine to screen calls.

☎ ***Leave complete messages:*** To reduce the tedium of telephone tag, leave as much detailed information as possible on someone else's answering machine.

☎ ***Leave clear messages:*** Whenever you leave a message on someone else's answering machine, include the best time to call you back. It's a sure-fire way to avoid being disturbed in the middle of bathing the baby.

☎ ***Last-minute leeway:*** Turn on your answering machine 15 minutes before you need to be out the door. That way, if any last-minute calls come in while you're getting ready, you won't be delayed.

☎ ***Record two messages:*** Prerecord one message for weekdays on one side of your answering machine tape and another for the weekend on the second if you want weekend callers greeted differently than weekday people.

☎ *Jog your memory:* If there's something you absolutely have to do when you get home, just call your answering machine and leave yourself a message. It's probably the first thing you'll check.

☎ *Human answering machines:* If you don't have an answering machine and you need a block of uninterrupted time, ask a family member or roommate to answer the phone for an afternoon or evening.

☎ *Kids taking messages:* If your children take phone messages for you, instruct them to write them down and to repeat names, spelling and numbers back to the callers so the information is recorded correctly.

☎ *Know your objectives:* Keep a memo pad near your phone and make it a habit to jot down the purpose of your calls before you make them. This way you won't forget something and then have to call back.

☎ *Note the outcome:* To remind you that you left a message on someone else's answering machine or with someone who answered their phone, enter "msg" (message) next to that person's name on your phone list.

☎ *Avoid interruptions:* Don't stop what you're doing to start phone calls or conversations that break your concentration.

☎ *Phone center:* Organize the space near all your phones to make and receive calls efficiently. Keep a pad next to every one, preferably with a pen or pencil on a cord that can be attached to the telephone itself.

☎ *Reduce runaround:* Keep your calendar, phone books, an area-code map and your personal address books close to the phone for easy reference. This eliminates scrambling around for what you need when you make your calls.

☎ *Time-saving calling:* Set aside a specific time during the day for making all your necessary calls at one sitting.

☎ *Limit conversations:* Keep your conversations focused on the subject at hand and save the schmoozing for when you have more time.

☎ *Preplan conversations:* Determine what you're going to say before making a complicated call about travel plans or prices of repair services. Note the date, name and number of the person you're calling and list the items you want to cover – in order of importance. Take notes during the conversation.

☎ *Shorten conversations:* Start each conversation with a reminder to be brief. Just say, "I only have a minute…"

☎ *Shorten calls altogether:* Learn to cut unwanted phone calls short by firmly saying "I'm busy right now."

☎ *Brief reminder:* Set a kitchen timer near the phone, and set it to ring after a reasonably short amount of time. When it rings, just say "Oops! My cake's done. Gotta go."

☎ *Unplug phone:* Turn off or unplug your phone whenever you don't want to be disturbed.

☎ *Free the phone:* Try to negotiate a time each day when the phone is off-limits to the kids. This will help to have the phone free when you need it.

☎ *Optimize phone time:* Get a 25-ft. phone cord so you can complete simple chores in the kitchen as you talk.

☎ *Cordless phone:* Go cordless. Now that they're cheaper, a cordless phone can be an amazing timesaver!

Other Rooms to Organize

THE BEDROOM

❖ *Closet expander:* Add a horizontal rod halfway down one side of your closet.

❖ *Link up space:* Hang a length of chain from a hanger. Each link can hold one hanger – which takes up much less storage space.

❖ *Add closet shelves:* If there's room in your closet, put a shelf at each end. If the shelf above the hanger rod has enough space, double-deck another shelf above it.

❖ *Closet door space:* Add several hooks to the inside of your closet door to hang belts, ties, small purses and lots of other little items.

❖ *Shoes:* Hang them from screw-in doorstops installed on the inside of the closet door.

❖ *Belts:* For a nifty belt holder, install a row of big cup hooks along the bottom of a wooden hanger.

❖ *Under the bed:* Attach casters to bins that fit under the bed to make convenient roll-out storage for linens, toys, etc. Clear plastic storage boxes with snap-on lids are especially great for storing seasonal clothing.

❖ ***Extra blankets:*** Eliminate the question of where to put extra blankets. Store them between the mattress and the box spring.

❖ ***Make that bed:*** Do it every morning. It gives the whole room a fresh, neat feeling, gives you a jump-start on feeling organized – and you won't be tempted to flop back into it!

❖ ***Closet clutter:*** Clear it out! If you haven't worn something in the past year, give it away. Discard or recycle anything that's old, out of style or doesn't fit. Put "maybes" in a separate pile. If after a month, you still have not worn it, give it away.

❖ ***Shoe bag storage:*** Use clear plastic hanging shoe bags as terrific organizers for bulky socks or hosiery.

❖ ***Hosiery bar:*** Store hosiery rolled up in a drawer, with similar colors together. Line them up from front to back. When you're ready to wear a pair, take the one in front and push the whole line forward. When putting away new or clean hosiery, place it in the back.

❖ ***Easy rehanging:*** Every time you take a hanging item from your closet, take out the hanger, too. Keep it on the closet door handle. This reminder makes it convenient to hang the garment back up when you undress.

❖ ***Underwear:*** Insert sectional dividers in your underwear drawer – and throw out all those old, worn undies.

❖ ***Jewelry hooks:*** Arrange hooks in a pleasing pattern on the bedroom wall and hang up all your necklaces and bracelets. It's not only pretty, but assures they'll stay untangled. Not enough wall space? Attach hooks behind the door.

❖ ***Small jewelry:*** Place an ice cube tray in a drawer to neatly hold your smallest accessories.

❖ *Night table clutter:* Keep a bowl or dish on your night table to collect all those doodads you take off when you sleep. This avoids that bleary-eyed morning hunt for your watch, ring, keys, wallet and spare change.

❖ *Color-coded closets:* Arrange your closet by color rather than by clothing type. It'll be much simpler to pull outfits together when dressing and it helps spot where your wardrobe needs filling out before you shop. Make four sections: whites, brights, pastels and darks.

❖ *Bundle bed linens:* For quick and easy bedmaking, keep linen sets together. For each set, fold and wrap a top and bottom sheet and extra pillowcases together. Then stick them all in a matching pillowcase and store.

❖ *Closet light:* Install one. Even if your closet is the most organized in the world, if you can't see into it, what's the use?

❖ *Hang loose:* Hang all your clothing far enough apart so they air out and don't wind up wrinkling each other.

❖ *Hang high:* Set a hanger pole high enough in your closet so your longest dresses or jumpsuits can hang freely.

❖ *A final check:* Clean off all lint or dust before hanging up your clothing.

❖ *Plastic hangers:* Invest in plastic hangers. They don't crease your clothing like wire ones do.

❖ *Categorize clothes:* If color-coding isn't your thing, this will also cut down the time it takes to search for clothes in your closet. Organize into dressy clothing, office wear, day wear and hanging-around clothes.

❖ *What to eliminate:* Toss that skirt you've never worn, those casualties of the perspiration war, and anything you now wouldn't be caught dead in.

❖ *Think vertical:* Stretch the space on walls or on the back of closet doors by installing grids to hold belts, purses, hats and anything that can hang.

❖ *Donate discards:* Give them to the Salvation Army or the United Way. It's tax deductible. Bringing them to a consignment shop can even earn you cash.

THE BATHROOM

❖ *Magazine rack:* Here's how to make one: If your bathroom vanity cabinet is near the toilet, install a towel rack onto the cabinet, about six inches from the floor. It'll hold your reading material in place.

❖ *Makeup organizers:* Check out those acrylic organizers you see in office supply or art stores. They're ideal for brushes, nail polish, etc.

❖ *Evict the "expired":* Empty out your bathroom cabinet completely. Throw out everything that has passed the expiration date.

❖ *Modify makeup:* Sort nail polish, perfume and lipstick collections by category and color. Use any duplicates first. Then replace only as you run out.

❖ *Shower caddy:* Get one for your shower. It's convenient for holding soaps, shaving cream, lotions, shampoos, conditioners, razors, etc.

❖ *Coat rack:* Put one in your bathroom if it's large enough. It will keep clutter off the floor and is just perfect for hanging guests' towels and bathrobes.

❖ *Hair dryer:* Park it on a simple S-hook hung from the side of a wire shelf.

❖ *Metal magnetism:* Attach a long magnetized knife rack to the side of your medicine cabinet to hold little metal objects like scissors, tweezers, shavers and bobby pins.

❖ *Protect jewelry:* Hang a decorative hook on the wall – away from the sink. Slip your watch and jewelry on it before washing up.

❖ *Towels:* Store them on a stack of narrow shelves above the toilet tank.

❖ *Toiletries:* Stockpile those you use every day on a single wire shelf in the bathroom.

❖ *Tower power:* In a large bathroom, install a floor-to-ceiling storage tower. Just set up a narrow divider between the sink and toilet with shelves, drawers or cabinets. This can also add some welcome privacy!

❖ *Wall dispensers:* Install a wall dispenser that conveniently holds liquid soaps, lotions and shampoos.

❖ *Shower doors:* Glass shower doors stay cleaner longer if you spray them lightly with furniture polish or lemon oil.

THE WORKSHOP AND GARAGE

❖ *Ever-ready noteboard:* Spray an ordinary window shade with chalkboard paint and mount it on the wall in front of your workbench. When you need to make a note of something, just pull it down.

❖ *Apartment workbench:* Cut some plywood to a good-sized work surface. Install a pair of wooden cleats underneath the board to hold it snugly over your kitchen sink. *Voila!* Best of all, it slips under your bed or couch until you need it.

❖ *Mock workbench:* Just cover a folding ironing board with a plastic dropcloth and go to work.

❖ *Garage space:* Paint a white boundary stripe on the floor of the garage to ensure that big items, like bikes and lawn mowers, stay safely out of the way of your car.

❖ *Garage wall storage:* Hang a shoe bag on a wall to hold dozens of stray items.

❖ *Bicycle:* Suspend your bike from a large hook in the ceiling.

❖ *Bike rack:* Make one out of an old iron headboard that has vertical posts. Set it in concrete with the bottom rail on the ground so that each bike's front wheel can slip in between the posts.

❖ *Parking guide:* Paint a luminous stripe on the end wall of the garage to guide your aim when you pull in.

❖ *Easy parking:* Attach an old tire to the wall at bumper level to remove the guesswork of how far to go into your garage. Or dangle a sponge-rubber ball on a string from the ceiling so it barely touches the windshield.

THE LAUNDRY ROOM

❖ *Hook-up hangers:* Hang a hefty hook in the laundry room near where you do your ironing. It's great for holding a batch of just-ironed clothing so you only make one trip to the closet.

❖ *Socks:* Give each family member a mesh lingerie bag for their own socks and underwear. When the bags come out of the dryer, sorting's a breeze.

❖ *Disappearing socks:* Safety pin socks together before doing the laundry.

❖ *Laundry emergency kit:* Keep some regular hair shampoo in your laundry room. Dab some on clothing with body-oil stains and let it stand awhile before washing.

ANYWHERE

❖ *Room use:* Insist on *no shoes* in the living room, *no plates* in the bedroom and *no games* in the kitchen. Otherwise, you'll wind up with extra work picking up from everywhere.

❖ *Create a task spot:* For one-stop tasking, set up a central station with all the necessary tools for the task within easy reach – whether it's for mailing packages, writing letters or doing laundry.

❖ *Follow the experts:* They know how to organize their specialties. If you collect books and records, visit a bookstore or music store. For art and knitting, stop into a specialty shop.

❖ *Velcro strips:* Attach one to the side of your TV set and another to the back of your TV remote.

❖ *Keep pens handy:* Assign them a specific place in every room, pocketbook and notebook so you never have to search for one. For the kitchen, get a magnetic pen that sticks to the fridge.

❖ *Serving bar:* Turn a little-used closet into a serving bar. Add a few shelves to hold glasses and slip in a junior-sized cabinet for worktop space, to stock bar items and to keep an ice chest handy.

❖ **Rack up space:** Put a coat rack in the guest room. It'll be more accessible than your overstuffed closet.

❖ **Message center:** Create a family message center everyone can check as soon as they come home. Attach an erasable board with a hanging marker on the fridge or keep a notepad and pen next to a "message box" in the family room.

❖ **Family "in-station":** Set up a spot where every family member can deposit mail, leave messages, etc.

❖ **Keys:** Use a pretty, decorative bowl on a table near the front door to hold house keys. You'll always know exactly where they are.

❖ **Color code books:** Stick a colored label on each spine: red for reference, purple for romance, etc. You'll be able to locate them at a glance.

❖ **Discard time:** Put those things you're uncertain about discarding into one box. If in a month it never even occurred to you to use any of it, get rid of them.

❖ **Jettison junk:** Check out that junk drawer. If you haven't a clue about what some thingamajig is, kiss it goodbye.

❖ **Keep things reachable:** Keep those things you need quickly or use most often in easy-to-reach areas, that is, at heights somewhere between midthigh to shoulder.

❖ *Rolling storage:* Buy a free-standing storage cart on wheels that can just roll out of sight. Great for the kitchen, laundry room or nursery.

❖ *Rugs:* Don't buy hard-to-clean carpets. Low pile is a better dust-buster than shag.

❖ *Desk sets:* Glue a cluster of several different short lengths of PVC piping together. Put end caps on the bottom and you have an organizer for pencils, pens and other invaluable office tools.

❖ *Outdoor storage:* If you're out of space, attach a second-hand school locker to a post in your carport. Just be sure you mount it with the fasteners inside.

❖ *Shelve the problem:* Add narrow open shelves to a long wall in the hallway from the floor all the way to within a foot of the ceiling.

❖ *Flexible shelving:* Install adjustable bookshelves only.

❖ *Wires:* Loop the long wires from computers, stereos, phones, etc. in neat circles over wall hooks installed behind the furniture.

❖ *Basement storage:* Transform the metal lally columns in your basement floor into circular shelf units. First, cut out round shelves with a hole for the pole. Then cut in half and use L-shaped brackets to attach them to the poles.

Get a Handle on Your Tools

☞ **Nuts & bolts:** Attach a screen-door handle in the center of a muffin pan. It makes an easy-to-carry hardware holder.

☞ **Borrowed tools:** Paint your tool handles bright red. Your neighbor won't ever forget who he borrowed that rake from. It's also super for spotting small tools in the garden.

☞ **Hacksaw blades:** Tape extra blades to the top of the hacksaw frame for convenient storage.

☞ **Socket wrenches:** Get a nut to fit each socket. Then glue the nuts in a row in a tool tray. Store each socket on its own nut.

☞ **Hang wrenches:** Slip wrenches onto one of those heavy-duty giant safety pins. You can hang an entire set on your workshop wall.

☞ **Razor blades:** To safely store single-edged razors, make a vertical row of slots in a workshop wall stud and slip the razors in. If you don't have exposed studs, glue a block of Styrofoam to the wall.

☞ *Ladder:* Nail a sturdy old leather belt to the garage wall. Store the ladder by wrapping the belt around its top step and buckling it closed.

☞ *Sandpaper:* Put a stack in a clipboard and hang that from a wall hook.

☞ *Sandpaper storage:* Store loose sheets of sandpaper in the cover of a record album. Tape a label on it to identify the contents.

☞ *Circular blades:* Stick circular saw blades in an old record album jacket.

☞ *Drill storage #1:* For quick retrieval, pack your drill and all the bits in an old lunch box.

☞ *Drill storage #2:* Stick an eyebolt into the drill and hand tighten it so the drill can hang from a hook.

☞ *Drill bits:* Keep a batch of small drill bits stored in a snap-lid glasses case near your drill.

☞ *Rolls of tape:* Don't toss out that old metal toilet-paper holder. Mount it on your workshop wall to hold a half-dozen types of tape in easy reach.

☞ *Small tools:* Attach a short length of gutter (with end caps attached) under a sawhorse to hold those tools and small items you need while you work.

☞ *Zigzag folding rule:* String a loop through your zigzag ruler and hang it from a hook.

☞ *Lumber:* Throw down a pile of old auto tires and store your lumber on top.

☞ *Loose screws, etc.:* Sort all those loose screws and tiny washers in a plastic ice cube tray.

☞ *Metal washers:* Hang a large safety pin from your workshop wall. It holds a hefty supply of metal washers.

☞ *Screwdrivers:* Tightly coil a roll of corrugated cardboard and stuff it into a 2-lb. coffee can. Poke all your screwdrivers between the corrugations.

☞ *Saw blade:* Use a clamp-on pants hanger to hold the end of a saw blade; then hang it on the wall.

☞ *Chicken wire grid:* If your garage or workshop has exposed studs, staple lengths of chicken wire across several of them. Add S-hooks for hanging all sorts of tools.

☞ *Door hinges:* Fold hinge sets together, with their screws outward, wrapped in a rubber band and store.

☞ *Glass cutter:* Store your glass cutter in a plastic toothbrush holder.

☞ *Moving that mower:* Attach a screen-door handle to the front of your rotary mower housing. It will be a whole lot easier to lift.

☞ *Wheelbarrow:* Mount a couple of large hooks or screws on the wall of your garage or shed and hang up your wheelbarrow. It will take up a lot less room.

☞ *General tool storage:* Use a permanent marker to outline each tool's shape in its place on the wall so you'll always know exactly where to return them.

☞ *Pill bottles:* Store all sorts of tiny parts in pill bottles. You can see the contents and retrieve them in a jiffy.

☞ *Vacuum cleaner:* Always keep a spare "shop vac" bag and belt on hand.

Eke Out More Minutes
Timesaving Tips

✪ *Mark belongings:* Stick a bright-colored tassel of yarn on luggage handles and the car antenna and you'll spot your suitcases or car in seconds.

✪ *Shopping list:* Onto each recipe that you prepare regularly, clip a list of the ingredients you usually need to buy for it. When you're ready to shop, pencil-check the items you're out of and note the amounts you need. When you're done shopping, erase the notations and return the list to your recipe book.

✪ *Time check:* If you're always late, set your clocks ahead 10 minutes.

✪ *Minimize morning chaos:* Connect your coffee maker to a timer (if it doesn't already have one) and set it so that your coffee is ready when you are in the morning.

✪ *Mailing labels:* Got a computer? Buy a simple software program for preprinting batches of labels for frequently used addresses. Keep them sorted alphabetically in a file right near where you handle your mail.

✪ *Instruction manuals:* Tape a copy of the manufacturer's booklet directly to the appliance and you'll never need to search for it.

❁ *Deductibles:* Keep a separate checking account for tax deductible expenses and sort them every month by category, such as charitable contributions, medical and dental expenses. By year end, you'll be way ahead in the tax preparation hassle.

❁ *Quick orientation:* When you arrive in a new place, first get an overview with an in-city bus tour. This avoids having to drive around in a strange place and pinpoints the places of interest you might want to explore later on your own.

❁ *Vacation pictures #1:* Buy rolls of slide film that come with mailers and pop them into a mailbox as you finish each roll. By the time you get home, your slides will be waiting there for you.

❁ *Vacation pictures #2:* Or, use those 60-minute film services to develop your film *before* you move on to your next stop. If important shots didn't turn out just right, you'll have time to reshoot.

❁ *Quick pick-up:* To pick up dropped nails, hold a magnet against one side of a lid from one of those plastic margarine containers so the nails are attracted to the lid's underside. Then simply place the lid over the container and remove the magnet.

❁ *Battery power:* Stock up on batteries when they're on sale. Store extras in the fridge.

❁ *Stockings:* Order discounted hosiery direct from the manufacturer for big savings of both time and money. A variety of brands are available from the hosiery hotline: 800-926-4022.

❁ *Don't waste commercials:* Do something productive. Start the laundry, wash the dishes, water the plants.

✿ *Set up routines:* Schedule routine tasks for the same time each day or week. For example, mop the kitchen floor on Monday; save ironing and shopping for Wednesday, etc. Then by the weekend, you can relax and reward yourself.

✿ *Chart your chores:* Make a pie chart to help you analyze what percentage of your time is spent at each task. It helps to pinpoint where the time goes so you can make adjustments when necessary.

✿ *No watched pots:* Do something while you're waiting for water to boil: Wash dishes, empty the dishwasher, set the table, etc.

✿ *The night before:* Accomplish as much as possible before you go to sleep. You'll sleep better – and confront less chaos in the morning – if the dishes are washed and the trash is on the curb.

✿ *Quick dress:* Lay out tomorrow's wardrobe tonight. Assemble everything – including accessories – and hang on a hook behind the door.

✿ *Pen tip:* When choosing a pen, select one with a clickpoint that requires only one hand to operate – without removing, storing and replacing a cap.

✿ *Trial-size products:* Leave a bunch packed and ready to go in a toiletries case in your suitcase. Include shampoo, conditioner, shaving cream, a razor, toothpaste, powder and hand cream.

✿ *Carry-on luggage:* If possible, avoid checking luggage when you travel by plane. You not only eliminate the risk of losing it, you save all that waiting time at the other end.

✸ *Seconds savers:* Screw on the toothpaste cap after brushing; pat the soap dish dry after using; wipe shoes before entering house; change out of your good clothing before fixing dinner; clean up spills as they happen.

✸ *Quick drying:* Add a few dry, clean, small towels along with the wet laundry you put into the dryer. The whole load will dry faster.

✸ *Read directions:* Whether you're assembling a prefabricated television cabinet or a child's bike, FIRST read through all the instructions.

✸ *VCR saves time:* Tape now and watch later so you don't sacrifice any quality time with family or interrupt a project just to catch a special program.

✸ *Commercial breaks:* Tape a show even if you have the time to watch it when it's broadcast. Fast-forwarding through the commercials saves you at least 10 minutes per show!

✸ *Television guide:* Highlight the programs you want to watch in the TV program guide. During the week, you'll see your choices at a glance without rereading the guide. Use a highlighter in another color for alternative choices.

✸ *Business card info:* Staple each business card right onto a Rolodex card. This saves repeating information that's already on the card. If necessary, trim to fit.

✸ *Get your bearings:* Keep a "directions" file and, whenever you take down directions to a place you're likely to visit again, just slip a note into the file.

✸ *Use commuter time:* Listen to educational tapes during long car trips or make tapes of your own by dictating ideas, letters, etc. into a voice-activated recorder. If you commute by train or bus, pay bills or read mail on the way.

❂ *Location, location, location:* Assign a permanent place to keep items you use often – and keep them there!

❂ *A holding pattern:* Mount a heavy-duty hook outside, close to your front door. You'll find it invaluable for temporarily hanging shopping bags or dry cleaning while you get out your house keys.

❂ *House key helper:* Get a long plastic key chain (it looks like a phone cord) and attach it to your purse handle. Then, no matter where in your pocketbook your keys are hiding, you'll always be able to reel them in by the chain.

❂ *Convenient banking:* Keep a pen, your bank card, deposit slips and a calculator with your checkbook. Then you can get in the bank line and write checks, fill out deposit slips and make entries in your register while you wait.

❂ *Simplify directions:* If you have frequent guests or have moved to a new home, write instructions to your home from the north, east, south and west, and include a sketched map. Keep a batch of photocopies to send future visitors.

❂ *Christmas lights:* If those sets of stringed lights wound up in a giant jumble because of last year's haphazard storage, plug in one set so that it lights. This will guide you more easily through the untangling.

❂ *Errand efficiency:* Organize your weekly errands geographically. You'll save a lot of valuable travel time as well as gas dollars.

❂ *Idle time:* Use unplanned blocks of time – such as in the doctor's waiting room – to answer letters or balance your checkbook.

❂ *Quick-dry nails:* To speed up the drying time of your nail polish, set your hands in a bowl of cold water when your nails are partially dry. The freezer (if you can stand it) is even better.

✪ **Nail polish bottles:** Rub petroleum jelly inside the cover of a new bottle of nail polish and on the grooves of the bottle so that it will always open easily.

✪ **Rise early:** To get an edge on your day, try to be showered and dressed well before your kids scramble into the kitchen for breakfast.

✪ **A.M. vs. P.M.:** Devote the mornings (when the kids are at school) to completing your chores. That way, you can save the afternoons for them.

✪ **Pack for unpacking:** If you pack your own bags at the supermarket, put similar items together: frozen foods, paper products, etc. This will save time unpacking, sorting and storing once you get home.

✪ **What's the hurry?** Don't pressure yourself unnecessarily. If you have to be somewhere (and it's not an emergency) can you arrive late and leave early?

✪ **Systemize marketing:** Make up your shopping list aisle by aisle in the supermarket. You won't waste time zigzagging back and forth.

✪ **Be flexible:** Reassess your routine on a regular basis, especially if it feels like you just don't have enough breathing space.

✪ **Ward off interruptions:** Quite simply, learn to say no!

✪ **Back seat reminder:** Throw clothes that need to go to the cleaners, library books to be returned, or packages that have to be shipped into the back seat of your car. They'll be ready whenever you're near where they need to be dropped off.

Trim Your Legwork
Step-saving Hints

➤ *Gifts:* If you give lots of presents, designate a certain type of gift for standard occasions, like crystal champagne flutes for engagements or cookbooks for dinner hostesses. Buy extras to keep on hand, wrapped and ready to go.

➤ *Survival kits:* Keep a beach bag permanently packed with sun hat, towel, lotion, beach umbrella, etc. – plus a list of things to add at the last minute, like your cooler or cassettes. Do the same for gym bags, suitcases or baby bags.

➤ *Lost items:* If you or your spouse forever lose or misplace stuff, take steps: Stock up on extra pens so that it'd be impossible not to find one. Having extra sets of house and car keys isn't a bad idea, either.

➤ *Thwart cooking mess:* Stick little plastic bags on your faucet handles before you start working with messy baking ingredients. All that flour and batter clings to the bags instead of the faucet handles.

➤ *Plastic bags:* When you're painting and need to leave the paint area, slip a plastic sandwich bag over your paint-splotched hands. It'll shield door knobs and everything else from your paint prints.

➤ *Remove all stains promptly:* Attack those nasty stains as soon as you possibly can. They are more likely to set permanently or be harder to get out if you don't.

➤ *Phone books:* When you arrive in a new city, check out the front of the local phone directory. It lists historical landmarks and other points of interest. It might even include a seasonal calendar of events and museum hours.

➤ *Recycling:* To make a one-step bundling bin for recycling newspapers, mount small handles opposite each other on two (inside) sides of a box. Cut a length of twine long enough to fit across the bottom, hook onto the cleats, and then some. When the box is full, unhook the string and tie up the stack.

➤ *Less lawn work:* Xeriscape to save water, mowing and fertilizing. This planting method combines mulched beds with ground cover, shrubs and trees that thrive naturally in your region.

➤ *Window washing:* Clamp a paper grocery bag to your belt with a clip-type clothespin when washing windows. It's nifty for holding the used paper towels or newspapers.

➤ *Trash bags:* Store a few extra plastic trash bags and

twist ties underneath the bag now in use. When it's full and you remove it, there's another one ready.

➤ *Roof tip:* Use binoculars for a bird's-eye view of your roof. Don't bother climbing all the way up to examine the flashing, shingles or tiles.

➤ *Drawers:* Store frequently used items in top drawers.

➤ *Trek trick:* Whenever you're serving food or drinks in any room other than the kitchen, use a tray. You'll save trips back and forth when serving and cleaning up.

➤ *Credit card correspondence:* Compose a form letter to your credit card company that includes standard information, like your account number, with blank spaces for specifics. Keep a photocopied supply handy.

➤ *Often-used items:* If you are a regular user of such things as scissors and Scotch tape or aspirin and hand cream, keep one in each of the rooms you need them in.

➤ *Pick up:* As you go from room to room, take something with you that needs putting away – whether a fresh tube of toothpaste for the upstairs bathroom or slippers left in the den. Set upstairs items at the foot of the stairs.

➤ *Economize movements:* Attach an extra-long extension cord to your vacuum cleaner. It will reduce the amount of times you have to plug and unplug it.

➤ *Wall groupings:* When arranging groups of anything on a wall, arrange each piece on an old sheet on the floor. Then outline each piece and tape the sheet to the wall. Use it as a guide for the nail holes. Remove sheet and hang the pieces.

➤ *Eyeglasses:* Invest in several inexpensive pairs of glasses and keep one in each room.

➤ *Extras on hand:* Buy staples like toothpaste, toilet paper, tissues, etc. in bulk. Make a note when you're running low.

➤ *Vital statistics:* Keep a list in your wallet of each family member's clothing sizes, color preferences and brand choices. This eliminates an extra trip just to exchange something that didn't meet expectations.

➤ *Canvas shoes:* Heavily spray your new pair of white canvas shoes with starch and they'll stay looking like new without having to clean them. Fabric protector also helps.

➤ *Ashtrays:* Polish ashtrays with furniture polish before using and they'll be a cinch to wipe clean.

➤ *Equip for cleaning:* To reduce your legwork when doing household chores, wear a work apron for carrying all the things you need. Tote heavier cleaning supplies in a lightweight plastic bucket.

➤ *Paper towel carrier:* Use a spare "plumber's friend" (toilet-bowl plunger) to hold your roll of paper towels as you go from room to room while cleaning. It conveniently keeps towels upright and ready-to-roll wherever you are.

➤ *Second bucket:* When working with liquid cleaners, use two buckets: one for the cleaner, the other for rinsing. That way, the cleaning solution always stays clean.

➤ *Dust less:* Keep your windows closed unless you delight in a refreshing breeze or you're airing out the house. It'll keep the dust down.

➤ *Easy-to-clean:* When buying furniture and accessories, select materials that are easy to clean such as Formica in the bathroom and PVC furniture in the family room. And remember, shower curtains are easier to clean than shower doors.

Others Can Help

THE KIDS

�֍ **Keep them occupied:** When traveling, take along plenty of modeling clay. Besides being fun, soft clay won't cause damage – even when Junior lobs it across a crowded lobby.

�֍ **Cure hang-ups:** Install rods low enough in your child's closet so that he or she learns to hang things up.

✤ **Safety:** Keep kids away from tools. Store them in a workbench drawer, then drill a hole through the top of the workbench just inside the back end of the drawer. Drop a bolt into the hole.

✤ **Keep watch:** To check your sleeping infant without making noise or waking her up, install a security-door viewer in the nursery door or replace the regular door altogether with a glass storm door.

⁂ ***Infants and pets:*** Install a screen door on a self-closing spring in the nursery. This way you can easily see – and hear – the baby. It also gives kitty a chance to get used to the baby while keeping his curiosity in check.

⁂ ***File it:*** Get some bright file crates, folders and labels and encourage the kids to set up a filing system. Suggest they record their buddies' birthday info, a party diary, rock star facts and photos, sports data or letters.

⁂ ***Label clothing:*** Label all your kid's clothing, especially those things they'll probably put down or remove (and then lose!) like eyeglass cases, book bags, gloves and hats.

⁂ ***Storage cubes:*** Organize toys, books and clothing in square storage cubes placed on their sides and stacked. If they're attractive and accessible, the kids are more likely to use them.

⁂ ***Color them organized:*** Set up a desk canister just for their art supplies.

⁂ ***Deter distractions:*** Keep paper and crayons handy in a kitchen drawer. The kids can concentrate on an arts and crafts project while you fix dinner.

⁂ ***Toss together:*** Pare down clutter with teamwork. At the end of each school year, ask your child to decide what to save. Store those and toss the rest. This helps teach organization and decision-making.

⁂ ***For tots:*** Teach your toddler to pick up his or her own toys, clothing and non-breakable dishes.

⁂ ***Chores:*** Teach kids to undress in their own rooms and hang up their clothing immediately; put dirty laundry in the hamper; break the ends off beans or pea pods, etc.

✻ *Mock mud room:* Make a mud room for removing dirty shoes and boots. For boots, use an old bath mat (or disposable foil trays); for dumping hats, snowsuits and gloves, keep a plastic laundry basket near the entry.

✻ *Make rules:* Teach your kids these simple rules: Put used dishes in the dishwasher or sink; put away what belongs to them; wipe the tub, shower or sink after using; and replace soap or toilet paper immediately if it runs out.

✻ *Family calendar:* Post a calendar in the kitchen. On it, write family appointments and special occasions. Consider it the family's central station, making sure everyone consults it before making commitments.

✻ *Double your duties:* Plan a story hour with your kids while the laundry is in the dryer.

✻ *Laundry depot:* Set up a long shelf in the laundry room with the name of each family member posted prominently on the edge. Keep each one's folded laundry above his or her name so they can pick it up and put it away themselves.

✻ *Imaginative problem-solving:* Put the baby into a playpen when nature calls and park it at the bathroom door.

✻ *In the shower:* Take your toddler into the shower with you. Use a ring with suction cups that she can hold onto while you tend to yourself.

❋ *Keep ready:* Be ready to go on a moment's notice. Keep a baby bag handy – packed with extra diapers, snacks, etc., and park the stroller near the door.

❋ *Easy sorting:* Teach kids to presort darks and lights so you don't have to do it at laundry time. Try keeping two hampers in the bathroom for this purpose.

❋ *Mother's helpers:* Let older children start dinner before you get home from work. They can easily wash salad greens or set the table.

❋ *Borrowed books:* Designate one spot on a bookshelf where the kids can keep library books and insist they be placed there after they're read. This saves rummaging through all their books to find the borrowed ones.

❋ *School readiness:* Have your kids pack their own knapsacks and organize their own homework the night before. This way everything they need for school is ready for their dash out the door.

❋ *Foil finicky eaters:* If your child refuses to eat anything but tuna salad for school lunches, don't get aggravated, get prepped. Keep a never-ending supply of the favorite food on hand.

❋ *Breakfast buffet:* Set out some healthful breakfast foods that family members can easily combine themselves. Try yogurt with granola, a variety of dry cereals, English muffins, jam and peanut butter.

❋ *Important numbers:* For those tense times when you're trying to track down your kids, keep a list handy of those oh-so-important phone numbers – their friends, teachers, counselors and coaches.

⁂ ***Teach table-setting:*** On a white paper place mat, outline shapes of a fork, knife, spoon, plate and glass. Then let your toddler toy with matching plastic items to the appropriate shape.

⁂ ***Train kids early:*** Set your two-year-old on the floor and scatter several small toys near her. Show her how to put each toy into a big box, then let her try it herself. Praise her often.

⁂ ***Lesson responsibility:*** Rather than asking the kids to help you clean up their mess, teach them to clean it up themselves.

⁂ ***Lost mittens remedy:*** Sew a long piece of yarn between every pair of gloves and mittens and slip it through the inside of their coat and out both sleeves.

⁂ ***Schedule shopping spree:*** Organize one day-long trip with your preteen each season. Set aside enough time to break for lunch.

⁂ ***Last-minute rush:*** Insist that your kids dress before they come to breakfast.

⁂ ***Extra writing space:*** Convert any door or wall into an erasable note pad with chalkboard paint. The kids'll love it.

⁂ ***Dressing themselves:*** As little ones grow, they love dressing themselves. But what a mess! Keep out some colorful wire storage baskets – one with underwear, one with socks – and he'll learn to dress without mussing up the drawers.

⁂ ***Creative crawling:*** Baby can crawl to her heart's content, without injury, if you stitch or glue the trimmed head of a cotton mop onto each knee of her jeans or overalls.

⁂ ***Keep chore score:*** Make a chore chart for your six-year-old. Award gold stars for every chore he completes: from setting the table to making his bed and completing homework on time. When the chart is filled with stars, reward him.

⁂ ***Helpful hands:*** When you cook and bake, ask your little one to tear salad greens, stir cake mixes and slosh measuring cups clean.

⁂ ***Instill independence:*** Ask your six-year-old to bring in the mail, empty the trash, load the dishwasher and feed the family pet.

⁂ ***Involve your toddler:*** After a snack or a meal together, invite your three-year-old to put her own plastic cup and dish on the counter while you handle the breakables.

⁂ ***Playtime:*** When your four-year-old has friends over, end their playtime a few minutes early to give everyone time to pitch in to clean up the room.

⁂ ***Workout:*** Rent one of those mother-and-child exercise videos so the two of you can enjoy working out together. Or bring your child with you to an exercise class.

⁂ ***Preteen partnerships:*** Do your "homework" while your teen does hers. Sit together at a table big enough for both of you. While she's busy with her homework, you do yours – bill paying, menu planning or catching up on reading.

⁂ ***Teen teachers:*** Ask your teenager to give you lessons on her computer. Let her help you set up your own file for keeping track of household information.

⁂ ***Teen cooks:*** Persuade your teenager to prepare a balanced dinner for the entire family once a week. Not only will this teach him survival skills, but you'll have one less meal to worry about.

⁂ ***Shopper's aid:*** As soon as your child is old enough to read, do the grocery shopping together, splitting up the list between you.

⁂ ***Kiddy kitchen aide:*** Let your young child share in organizing the kitchen. Invite her to practice her learning skills by letting her alphabetize your spices.

✹ ***Set out clothing:*** Put out your children's school clothes the night before.

✹ ***Winding down time:*** When you get home from work, take your child out for a stroll. You'll score a triple: winding-down time for you, quality time with the kids and exercise for both of you.

✹ ***Back-up sitter:*** The last-minute news that your regular baby sitter can't make it doesn't have to be an inconvenience for you. Always be sure you've got a back-up waiting in the wings.

✹ ***Outgrown garb:*** Keep an empty box under your infant's crib. As she outgrows her clothing, stockpile them in the box. When the box is full, store in your attic or give it away.

YOUR SPOUSE OR ROOMMATE

✹ ***Spouse help:*** Ask your spouse to help you out more around the house. It usually works (but it might not always last).

✹ ***Trade off:*** If you've surprised him by taping a TV program you knew he'd enjoy seeing, ask him to put away one thing for every commercial he could fast-forward through.

✹ ***Think fast:*** If he says he doesn't have time to put the kids to bed because he wants to watch his favorite TV program, offer to free him up by taping it – then watch it later together.

✹ ***Negotiate:*** Swap drudgeries. Trade a list of three things you can't stand to do for three things he can't stand to do. You may not always like what you get in exchange, but at least it'll be different!

✹ *Swap skills:* Teach him how to iron a shirt in exchange for a lesson in using an electric drill. Set up the iron and ironing board near the TV so he can do it while watching the baseball game.

✹ *Tool use:* Let him see how easy it is to operate the food processor. While you're at it, show him how to clean it, too!

✹ *Hamper his style:* Put a clothes hamper right in his closet. Now there's no excuse for dropping that sweaty sweatshirt on the floor!

✹ *Just one meal:* Every week, delegate the preparation of one microwaveable meal to him. Start out simple: Let him reheat leftovers.

✹ *Convenient coupon clipper:* When he settles down with the Sunday sports pages, hand him the coupon inserts, too. Ask him to clip items you can use.

✹ *Menu plan together:* Set aside some time together to plan the week's menu and to prepare a shopping list. As you sort through the fridge and pantry, call out the groceries you need while he jots them down on the list.

✹ *Take turns:* Target responsibilities that are easy to divvy up, like taking turns arranging for baby sitters.

✹ *Pay tribute:* Reciprocate for all his help. If he has a sweet tooth, surprise him with his favorite dessert.

✹ *Mr. Chef:* If he considers himself a baron of the barbecue, feed his ego. Plan grilled main courses for dinner as often as possible – even in cold weather.

✹ *Stroke his ego:* He'll be sure to keep helping you if you do. Be sure he's eavesdropping when you tell your friends how great he's been around the house.

Remember the Small Things
Keeping Track

•→ *Mail orders:* Clip the catalog pages of your items and staple a note with information such as reference number, date you placed the order, etc. Note on your calendar the date it's expected to arrive.

•→ *Smoke alarms #1:* Do this twice a year. To make it easy to remember, coincide the battery test with the start and end of Daylight Savings Time.

•→ *Smoke alarms #2:* If your smoke alarms are battery operated, change batteries at least once a year, regardless of whether or not they've been used. How to keep track? It's easy. Synchronize battery changes with your birthday.

•→ *Circuit breakers:* Trip and reset circuit breaker switches once a year. Any corrosion that goes unnoticed can prevent it from tripping when you need it. Schedule this checkup on the same day you change smoke alarm batteries.

•→ *House check:* To avoid surprise breakdowns, make a periodic tour of appliances and furniture and tighten every nut, bolt and screw you can get to.

•→ *Household chemicals:* Date stamp any chemicals that

have a limited shelf life. Knowing when they were purchased lets you use up the oldest ones first.

→ *Venetian blinds:* If you're interrupted in the middle of cleaning Venetian blinds, pinpoint where you leave off by clipping a clothespin onto the last slat you cleaned.

→ *Yardstick tip:* When measuring with a yardstick, slip a rubber band around the ruler. It functions as a sliding marker to help keep the place you just measured.

→ *Measurement memo:* Stick a strip of masking tape onto one arm (not the one you write with) for jotting down measurements. This way, they won't get misplaced while you work.

→ *Remembering sequence:* Dictate into a cassette recorder as you're disassembling an appliance. Then play back the tape to guide you through the reassembling. Or, place the removed parts – in sequence – on a wide strip of tape instead.

→ *Word-of-mouth:* To make perfect repairs, first read the instructions into your tape recorder. Then simply play it back as you work, pausing the recorder as necessary. Try this with recipes, too.

→ *Loose beads:* To keep beads in order while you restring them, arrange them on a strip of sticky tape.

→ *CDs:* If your CD or record player stacks multiple disks, stack the empty containers in playing order for easy replacing.

→ *Cable channel chaos:* Clip out one copy of the cable channel list from the Sunday paper and post it on the side of your TV with double-sided tape.

→ *Today's date:* Flag the current date in your appointment calendar with a bookmark so you don't have to hunt for today's page.

↪ *Car service:* In your glove compartment, store a chart of your car service and repairs. Enter the name of the repair station, type of service and mileage. Jot down in your appointment book the date of the next recommended service.

↪ *Feed the meter:* To know when to feed the parking meter, get a meter timer at any hardware or auto store, keep a small kitchen timer handy in the glove compartment, or set your watch alarm.

↪ *Baby's schedule:* Set the alarm on your watch to beep when it's time for baby's bath or feeding. You can even use this to remind you when it's time for a pediatric appointment.

↪ *Screw cue:* When tightening or loosening screws, remember: Left is loose, right is tight.

↪ *Work-safety reminder:* Keep a foam head made for wigs in a prominent place near your tools. On it, keep a hard hat, goggles, ear plugs and a face mask and you'll never forget to wear protective gear when you're working at home.

↪ *Paint cleanup:* When painting outdoors, keep a container of solvent and a supply of clean rags near the entrance to your house. This will remind you to clean up before you step inside.

↪ *Wall grouping layout:* Before repainting your walls, take a snapshot of your arrangement of trinkets so you can rehang them in minutes as soon as the paint dries.

↪ *Too many keys:* If you carry lots of keys, use colored

stick-on circles to identify them. Or color code them with nail polish.

➥ *Car tricks:* Keep a note taped to the driver's side door handle to remind you of all those important little things you tend to forget when you exit the car: turn off lights, remove keys from the ignition, take the tape deck.

➥ *Take-home reminder:* Store those perishable dinner items you picked up during your lunch break in the office fridge. You'll never forget to take them home if you put your car keys on top of the package!

➥ *Last-minute reminder:* Tack a note onto the inside of the front door and you'll never forget to take care of those little things before leaving the house. It'll jog your memory to turn off the A/C, take out the garbage, etc.

➥ *Front-door valet:* Attach a large clasp to a hook on the inside of the front door. Hang or clip whatever you need to take with you to complete all your errands: the checkbook and deposit slip, clothes for the cleaners or shopping list.

➥ *Videotape returns:* As soon as you've finished viewing a videotape, lean it against the inside hinge of the front door.

➥ *Eggs:* Can't remember if that egg in the fridge is cooked or raw? Spin it. If it wobbles, it's raw; if it spins easily, it's hard-boiled.

➥ *Morning call:* If you're the sort who "doesn't do mornings" but absolutely must make an important call when you wake up, stick a note to the bathroom sink or on the telephone.

➥ *Locate location:* If you can't keep track of where you store things, create a file – either on paper or computer – called "Where Is...?" and enter every important paper or piece of jewelry you've stashed.

↪ *Don't lose count:* Always count everything you're carrying – shopping bags, luggage, even cameras and coats. Then each time you stop and start up again, take a recount.

↪ *Gift-ability:* Set up a gift file. In it, note preferences your friends and loved ones have mention in passing – such as that best-selling novel your hubby would like to read, or your son's newest favorite rock group.

↪ *Photo note pad:* Each time you snap a picture, enter the picture's number, the date, place and subject. This list corresponds to the order your photos are in when you get them back, so the task of remembering is done!

↪ *Photos:* If you forget the previous tip, as soon as your photos are processed, identify them. While the memories are still fresh in your mind, jot on the back of each photo who, what, when, where and maybe even why.

↪ *Travel arrangement file:* In it, put a list of things you need to remember: special diets on the plane, reminders to use your frequent flyer number, car rental, hotel and airline phone numbers, etc.

↪ *Paint:* Before opening a new can, write the name, color and lot number on the bottom. Since that's the spot least likely to get covered with paint drips, it will be easy for you to read if you need to buy more.

↪ *Paint gauge:* Before resealing that paint can, paint a line on the outside of the can at the level of the remaining paint so you'll know at a glance how much you've got.

Gardening Goodies

❀ *Speedy seeding:* Make a "dibble" from 1-in. PVC piping cut long enough so you can stand straight when you grasp the top end (3- or 4-ft. long.) Cut one end at a steep angle. To make the hole, poke the pointed end into the ground. Plop the seed down the pipe's hollow center into the ground. Push the soil back into place.

❀ *Seed collecting:* Zip through the job of collecting seeds for replanting. Put a plastic bag over the bygone plant before digging it up. Shake vigorously and the bag captures all the seeds.

❀ *Pea picking:* Use your thumb and forefinger to grab each pod just below the stem – and pinch it off in one step. That way you won't have to pick off the stems when it's time to cook them.

❀ *Carpenter's apron:* Wear one (with pockets) when you garden. It's terrific for holding seed packets and keeping small tools handy.

❀ *Easy watering:* Lay down a soaker hose or sprinkler in the garden and leave it in place for the entire season, turning on when necessary.

❀ *Mailbox tool depot:* Buy a large weatherproof mailbox. It's roomy enough to hold all your gear: hand cultivator, shears, seed packets, etc. Stake it in the ground near a hedge or under a tree.

❁ *Twine holder:* Poke a trowel into the ground so the handle becomes a holder for the spool.

❁ *Dig just right:* Put a temporary but visible mark on the lower handle of your digging tool to indicate how deep you want the hole to be. Dig the hole until you've reached the mark you had indicated.

❁ *Eyeball your produce:* When they're small, stake the ground nearest the roots of fruits and vegetables such as squash and melons that grow into tangly masses. This way you can easily locate the main stem when they're ready for picking.

❁ *Hoses:* Install wire croquet-type wickets at the corners of your house and around flower beds. This protects your plants as you pull the hose around the garden. It also protects your hose from sharp edges.

Access Is Everything

✠ **Label boxes:** Whenever you stash anything in a storage box, label the contents as specifically as possible.

✠ **Closets:** Improve the light conditions in a dark closet by painting the walls with glossy white enamel.

✠ **Circuit breaker:** Carefully label your circuit breaker to indicate exactly which electrical items correspond to which switch.

✠ **Emergency flashlight:** Mount a wall magnet near your circuit breaker box strong enough to hold a flashlight in place. It will come in handy during a power failure.

✠ **Basement flashlight:** Keep a flashlight mounted near the bottom step so you can safely find your way during a power outage.

✠ **Safety flashlight:** Stick a magnetized flashlight onto the metal frame of your bed so you won't be in the dark if you hear strange noises in the night.

✠ **Paint toucher-upper:** Store a little leftover paint in a thoroughly cleaned shoe-polish bottle — the kind that has that little dauber brush in the cap.

✠ **Balance a recipe:** When cooking from a loose recipe page, prop it up this way: Stand a fork in a glass so its tines stick up and weave the recipe page between the tines.

✠ *Hard-to-see:* If you can't easily glimpse what's hidden in a hard-to-reach spot, use a hand mirror to scout it out. This goes for garage and shop shelves, too.

✠ *Baby towel:* Mount a towel bar on the back of baby's highchair. You'll find it invaluable for keeping a towel or wet rag handy for quick cleanups.

✠ *Fishing license:* For safekeeping, roll it up into a plastic toothbrush holder. Or, keep it in an empty pen barrel and clip to your shirt pocket.

✠ *Boating safe-deposit:* Put your watch, billfold and other valuables into plastic bag. Keep the bag in an empty coffee can with a snap-on lid. This will keep them dry and they'll float if your boat takes on water.

✠ *Nozzles:* Mount a broom clip on the outside wall of your house closest to the water source for your hose. It makes a convenient holder for the nozzle. Or, drive a nail only partway into the wall, then just slip the nozzle over it.

✠ *Hosiery:* Devise some system of knotting stockings and pantyhose so you can tell at a glance which are in perfect condition and which should be worn under pants. Suggestion: Knot the good ones in the center, the torn ones at the toe.

✠ *Buttons:* To easily find buttons in a jar, pour them into a dustpan. Not only is it easier to sift through to find what you're looking for, but it's a snap to pour them all back into the jar.

✠ *Extra buttons:* When any clothing item you buy comes with extra buttons, run a safety pin through the packaging and loop it around the hanger you keep the garment on.

✠ *Belts:* Loosely tack matching belts to the center of the dress, jacket, coat or robe it belongs to.

✚ *Barbecue:* Set it near the kitchen door and use it all year long.

✚ *Holiday stuff:* Round up items you only need for special occasions, like holidays. Store the stuff in separate boxes and mark accordingly. Designate some accessible but out-of-the-way place to keep all the boxes together.

Survival Kit for the Medicine Cabinet:

Check out your medicine cabinet. If someone in your house gets sick, could you get your hands on what you need in a jiffy? If your medicine cabinet is typical (a mess, that is), the answer is probably not.

So get organized now. First, carefully dispose of all expired medications. Then be sure your medicine cabinet is stocked with these essentials:

- **Ace bandage** (3-4 in. wide) – to wrap a sprain
- **Adhesive bandages** – to protect small, open cuts
- **Antibiotic ointment** – to combat skin infections
- **Antihistamine** (like Benadryl) – to relieve allergy attacks
- **Antiseptic** (like Betadine) – to kill germs in wounds
- **Aspirin** (or Tylenol) – to relieve pain
- **Cortisone cream** – for skin irritations and rashes
- **Gauze and tape** – to bind wounds
- **Pepto-Bismol** – for upset stomach
- **Syrup of ipecac** – to stimulate vomiting
- **Thermometer**

While you're at it, it's a good idea to assemble two portable first-aid kits for emergency preparedness – one for the house, the other for your car.

✥ *Quick change:* Before starting out on a trip, be sure you've got lots of change for making phone calls and dollar bills for tipping.

✥ *Spare change:* Always keep some spare change in your car for hungry meters and emergency phone calls. If you're not a smoker, use the ashtray to hold the money.

✥ *Travel bag:* Whenever you're traveling by air, pack a bag just for the plane. In it, stick a pair of cotton socks, bottled water, some fruit or a snack, foam earplugs, sunglasses, a book or magazine to read and your headset.

✥ *Jumper cables:* Lay jumper cables side by side and tape them together at two or three places. This will keep them untangled so they'll be ready to use whenever you need them.

✥ *Handy tote:* Convert a six-pack into a mini-toolbox. When the cans are empty, carefully remove the tops and stick them back into the plastic rings. It'll keep anything separated – from nails to paintbrushes.

✥ *Hammers:* To improvise a hammer holder, cut the loops of a six-pack into two pieces with three holes each. Slip one loop over your belt, putting a second through it to make a slip knot. The loop that hangs down holds the hammer at your side. Or, sling the loop over a ladder rung while you work.

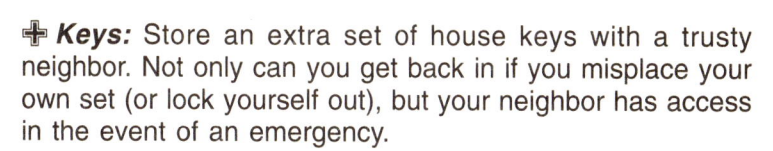

✥ *Keys:* Store an extra set of house keys with a trusty neighbor. Not only can you get back in if you misplace your own set (or lock yourself out), but your neighbor has access in the event of an emergency.

✥ *Trip directions:* Before a car trip, use a highlighter to mark your route on the map. Cut out the highlighted parts and number them in sequence. Wrap a rubber band around your car's visor and slip in the map part you currently need.

✚ **Computers:** Use it to: plan meals, search for recipes, create a cookbook, convert measurements, generate shopping lists, organize photo and slide collections and simplify bookkeeping. A program called *Sidekick* has an alarm that buzzes even when the computer is off.

✚ **Calendars:** Keep a calendar, whether on your desk or your wall. Why not give the kids one of their own? Also keep a datebook in your pocket for making those impromptu arrangements.

✚ **Moving:** When you pack, color code each box according to the room it should go in. Give the list to the movers.

✚ **Unpacking ease:** Lay a piece of kite string across each box where the sealing tape will eventually go. Leave a few inches of string sticking out on each end. When you get to your new home, just pull the strings to zip open the boxes.

✚ **Telephone directories:** Keep records in your phone books. Write in them, highlight them, add stickums, circle numbers you look up often, cross out those you never want to call again, correct mistakes, even tear out pages you want to keep permanently.

✚ **Tools on ladder:** Glue magnets around the edge of the top step of a ladder and frame the top step with pieces of molding to prevent small parts and tools from rolling off while you work. Suspend a basket from the ladder's fold-out shelf.

✚ **Sawhorses:** Glue a yardstick to the top rail of your sawhorse and you'll always be ready to make a quick measurement without hunting for the ruler.

Novel Ways to Cut Clutter

✷ *Straw basket:* Display colorful soaps in the guest bathroom in an old straw basket.

✷ *Shovel:* If that rusty old shovel has a "D" shaped handle, cut it off to a convenient length and sharpen one end. It makes a dandy garden dibble.

✷ *Tube it:* Cut an old inner tube to make a sleeve that will stop tire chains rattling around in your car trunk. Tape shut one end, drop in the chains and close the other end with a rubber band.

✷ *Door:* Use an old slab door as a tabletop or workbench surface for extra work space.

✷ *Wood hanger:* Hang a batch of paper grocery bags with a wooden clamp pants hanger. Just hang it from a nail until you need a bag.

✷ *Wire basket:* Hang the three-level variety in the bathroom for washcloths and soap or in the kids' room as a catch-all for their small toys and art supplies.

✷ *Shoe bags:* Use them in the garage to store tools, fishing lures and golf balls. Behind the kitchen door, store spices, baking utensils, etc., or fill with hats, mittens, toys.

✷ *Wastebasket:* Set a wastebasket in a closet to hold umbrellas, sporting equipment or rolls of gift wrap.

✳ *Flatware organizer:* Set a plastic organizer for silverware in your junk drawer, desk drawer, the sewing room or on top of the bathroom vanity and you'll never again have to grope for a pen, needles or makeup brush.

✳ *Nylon stockings:* Hang an old nylon stocking inside a pantry or a closet off the kitchen. It's perfect for storing potatoes and onions, as long as it doesn't have gaping holes in it.

✳ *Wooden spools:* Turn them into cutlery holders. Line up a row of spools so they're touching each other, then glue together. Mount them (bottom sides to the wall) inside a kitchen cabinet door. The knife blade slips through the natural gaps, while the handle rests on the spools.

✳ *Belts:* Suspend a pair of old belts from your attic rafters to hold a rolled-up rug. Tape a large coffee can to each end to keep pests from nesting inside.

✳ *Rubber gloves:* Cut rubber gloves into assorted-sized rubber bands. Be sure to cut the entire glove – even the fingers, which make great ponytail bands.

✳ *Wire hangers:* Tightly tape two or more flimsy wire hangers together to make them super-strong.

✳ *Newspaper:* Tightly roll sections of newspaper, band them with wire and use as fireplace logs.

✳ *Old newspaper:* Shred or wad old newspapers for packing material. They're great protection when tucked around breakables.

✳ *Coffee cans:* To make your own carryall for tools, join four coffee cans together with small nuts and bolts. Improvise a handle from a section of rope or a plastic clothesline.

✳ *Wicker trunk:* Stuff a wicker trunk with years of important files, the kids' toys or your out-of-season clothing.

✹ *Blue jeans:* Whip up a shop apron from an old pair of jeans. Cut out an apron shape from the rear-end section so the rear pockets are in front. Sew up the bottom and add some of the leftover material to the existing waistband to make a ribbon tie.

✹ *Photo album:* Store recipes or organize your stamp collection in an old photo album.

✹ *Hose storage #1:* The best way to store a hose is rolled up. Mount seven 2-lb. coffee cans to the garage wall with large screws. Center one can, then arrange the others in a circle around it, with the open ends facing out. The hose wraps around the outside. Use the cans for storage.

✹ *Hose storage #2:* Attach two coffee cans to adjacent wall studs. Just coil the hose in a figure eight.

✹ *Hose storage #3:* Hold a coiled hose in an old tire. Then simply roll the tire and the hose wherever you need to use the hose.

✹ *Hose storage #4:* Coil a small hose around a wooden coat hanger and hang from the wall.

✹ *Golf bag:* Use an old golf bag to haul yard tools. The pockets are perfect for small tools and garden gloves. Even if you don't use the bag for hauling tools, it makes a great place to store them.

✹ *Photocopies:* Write notes, send faxes, etc. on the backs of old photocopied pages. Keep them handy in a tray marked "Scrap."

✹ *Glove:* Convert a worn-out glove into a handy holster for small tools. Cut off the fingers and make two slits near the wrist so your belt can slip through. Drop the tools into the finger openings.

Innovations for Entertaining

❊ **Extra storage:** When entertaining a crowd, stand a tri-panel screen in a U-shape and stick a metal towel bar across the top for coat and hat storage. Or, on catty-corner walls, screw in a pair of eye hooks and connect a chain.

❊ **Planning portions:** If you're serving one entree or meat dish, allow 6 oz. for each guest. If you're giving them a choice of meat, fish and poultry, let's say, figure you'll need 2 oz. of each per person.

❊ **Prepare a menu:** If you do this when having large dinner parties, you won't forget to serve something. Keep the menu in plain sight, such as on the fridge.

❊ **Party salad:** To dry large amounts of salad greens, stick one cotton pillowcase inside another and fill with trimmed, washed greens. Fasten, toss into the washer with a large clean towel and set on "spin." After a few minutes, transfer leaves to a dry, clean pillowcase and store in the fridge. They'll stay perfect for 24 hours.

❊ **Whipped cream:** Use unflavored gelatin to firm up whipped cream. For each cup of heavy cream, dissolve 1 tsp gelatin in 2 Tbs hot water. Add while whipping and the cream will keep for several hours refrigerated.

❊ **Self-help guests:** Keep a handy selection of local guidebooks, maps, restaurant reviews, menus, bus and subway info, and recent local newspaper entertainment sections for out-of-town guests who want something to do.

THE WELL-STOCKED PANTRY:

Don't let the surprise arrival of drop-in guests get you down. Keeping a few simple basics on hand lets you whip up something out of nothing.

Here are some of the magic ingredients:

Rice: It pretty much feeds the world, so why not your guests, too? Great as a base for casseroles. Just add canned meat, fish or any leftovers.

Pasta: Ditto for pasta. It tastes super in soups and casseroles or tossed with meat, leftover chicken and vegetables.

Instant mashed potatoes: A natural as a side dish; but inject more pizzazz by mixing with canned fish or cooked vegetables. Fried up, this concoction makes a great main dish or party hors d'oeuvre.

Buttermilk baking mix: Wonderful for whipping up pancakes, biscuits, coffeecakes or dumplings.

Cream of mushroom soup: An ideal base for quick vegetable soups or casseroles. Thin with milk or wine for a tasty fish or poultry sauce.

Tomato sauce: A jiffy sauce starter for spaghetti or pizza. Mix with canned beans for chili, or use as a soup base.

Frozen green beans and peas: For a speedy side dish, defrost, drain and toss with herbs. Great for stretching a casserole or tossed into salads.

Kidney beans: Makes a terrific meatless-chili starter. Add to soups or mix with quick-cooked rice for a low-cost, high-protein main dish.

Zip Through Chores

🐌 Cluster tasks: While you're out, pick up those shirts for the kids and that prescription from the pharmacy, drop off the vacation film for developing and still get back in time to pick up your mate from the railroad station.

🐌 Batch chores: Don't answer one letter until you have a few to write, then do them all at one sitting. Likewise when you need to go to the copy shop, try to wait till you have a bunch to do.

🐌 Oil splatters: Sprinkle a little salt or flour into the pan before frying foods and there'll be less to wipe off your stove top.

🐌 Off-hours chores: Try not to do your chores during lunchtime, rush hours, Fridays and just before holidays.

🐌 Medical appointments: Ask your dentist or doctor when their least busy times are – and schedule your appointments then. You'll save many precious hours of waiting time.

🐌 Lunch break: Schedule it earlier – or later – than the normal lunch break of noon-to-one o'clock and your favorite restaurant will be less jammed.

🕭 *Shopping list:* On the fridge door, keep a running list of groceries you need as you think of them. Jot down items *before* they run out. And don't forget to take the list with you to the market!

🕭 *Permanent list:* Just once, go down each aisle of your supermarket with a pad and pencil. Jot down everything you usually buy, including size. Redo the list at home, adding blank lines after each section and at the end. Photocopy a batch and use one every time you or a family member shop.

🕭 *Gift shortcut:* When shopping for several gifts at once, prepare the cards ahead of time. On each envelope, put the address and your return address; under each flap, jot down in pencil the gift you want to buy. (Remember to erase it.) Take the cards with you and as you choose each gift, enclose the card and have the store send it.

🕭 *Window washing:* When washing windows, slip your drapes or curtains through a hanger, then hang it from the curtain rod to keep them out of your way.

🕭 *Venetian blinds:* To clean Venetian- or mini-blinds in half the time, saturate a cloth with rubbing alcohol, wrap it around a rubber spatula – and you'll be able to wipe both a top and a bottom slat clean at the same time.

🕭 *Drapery hooks:* To weave drapery hooks into fabric, stick each hook into a bar of soap before you insert it and it'll glide right in.

🕭 *Needle threading:* To easily thread a needle, spray your fingertip with hair spray or spray starch, then rub the end of the thread.

🕭 *Easy egg separating:* Crack the egg over a funnel. The white will run through while the yolk remains behind long enough for you to remove it.

Artificial flowers: Clean them quickly by pouring some salt into a paper bag large enough to hold the flowers. Add the flowers and shake vigorously. The salt absorbs all the dust and dirt.

Chandeliers: To clean chandeliers, wear a pair of cotton work gloves and dip your fingers into ammonia water. Then simply rub the chandelier clean with your hands.

Group interruptions: Schedule a number of repairs for the same day. Narrow down the distractions even further by limiting the appointments to just morning or evening.

Making the bed: Do it left to right – or the opposite. Either way, complete one entire side first. This saves having to go around it twice.

Dusting: Dust a room in one continuous flow.

Right tools: When cleaning bathtubs, use a wide brush with a handle instead of a cloth. It gives you more scrubbing power and also eliminates bending.

Glass cleaning: Use old newspapers for windows, mirrors or glass doors. They're lint-free, so you'll work less.

Preprep foods: When you return from the market, split up family-size meat packages into meal portions. Clean and slice, dice or chop fresh vegetables before storing – if you don't mind a small loss in vitamins.

Dishwashing: Unless you've left dishes in the sink overnight, simply scrape off loose food before loading plates in the dishwasher. If you load correctly, the right amount of soap and hot-enough water means you don't need to pre-rinse them.

Light lightens chores: To see what you're drilling, attach a pen light to the top of your drill with a rubber band. It'll shed light where you need it.

🦆 *Dirty dishes:* If food has already hardened on those unrinsed plates and pots, pour boiling water on them or fill the sink with water and let stand overnight.

🦆 *Trash collecting:* Carry one giant plastic bag and, beginning from the room farthest from the outdoor garbage can, go through the house just once.

🦆 *Garbage liner:* Leave a few fresh pail liners folded at the bottom of each garbage pail or trash basket. When you dump the garbage, a new liner will always be lying in wait underneath.

🦆 *Errand pool:* In return for your picking up some baby formula for your neighbor at the market, she might be willing to return some library books for you.

🦆 *Shop by catalog:* This saves an enormous amount of time. Just buy something from one catalog and you'll automatically get on the mailing lists of dozens more.

🦆 *Glass cleaner:* Fill a spray bottle with water and add 3 Tbs ammonia and 1 Tbs white vinegar.

🦆 *Whipping cream:* When whipping cream with an electric beater, cut two holes in the center of a sheet of waxed paper. Slip the beater stems through these holes before attaching them to the mixer. This way, the mixer stays clean.

🦆 *Milk-film remedy:* When scalding milk, rinse the saucepan in cold water first. It'll be much easier to clean afterward.

🍂 **No-watch noodles:** Turn off the heat as soon as you add the noodles to the boiling water. Let stand for 20 minutes. Your noodles won't stick and won't overcook and you don't need to watch the pot.

🍂 **Beach-toy cleanup:** For swift sand removal when you're at the beach, take a washable mesh bag along with you. When it's time to head home, just chuck all the kids' beach toys into the bag and rinse the whole thing in the ocean.

🍂 **Checking oil:** Save the guesswork when checking your car's oil by making the dipstick easier to read. Drill tiny holes at the lines that read "full" and "add" so they'll never get obliterated.

🍂 **Oil applicator:** Keep an ear-drop bottle filled with lubricating oil for small household jobs. The dropper easily gets oil into the tiniest spots – without mess.

🍂 **Wall arrangements:** If you're putting together a complicated wall arrangement, don't wait until it's all hung to discover you don't like it. Organize it first on the floor. Then starting at one corner of the grouping, measure the spaces between each piece, transfer those measurements to the wall and hang away.

🍂 **De-fat poultry:** Trim fat while the meat is partially frozen.

🍂 **Cheese grater:** Wipe it with oil before using and you'll glide through the cleanup afterward.

Efficiency Can Save You Money

✘ *Financial records:* Each month, separate all receipts into three #10 envelopes marked "household," "business-related" and "auto & travel." Keep each month's envelopes in a separate file folder. At year's end, you'll have a precise record for planning next year's budget.

✘ *Check register:* Begin each year with a new register. At the end of every month, start a new page. This reduces the chances of making duplicate payments, makes it easier to look up old payments, and smooths the path for tax preparation.

✘ *Balance checkbook:* Balance your checkbook as soon as your statement arrives each month.

✘ *Check-writing:* Enter all the necessary information in your register before you write the check. That way, you'll never forget.

✘ *Credit cards:* Instead of making a list of your credit card numbers, photocopy them. It's easier. And if you photocopy the backs as well, you'll have those important phone numbers handy in case of loss or theft.

✗ *Credit lines:* Keep a running balance of your credit line. When you've reached the limit on your credit card, leave home without it.

✗ *Credit card charges:* Check your credit card receipts against your bill as soon as it arrives and notify the company immediately if there are any discrepancies.

SET UP A BUDGET:

Living on a budget doesn't mean living with less than you'd like; it means deciding how to keep more for the things that matter most. By juggling where you spend, you should be able to put away small enough increments each month to help you meet your family's long-term goals.

1) First list all your income and all the outgo, the major categories where you spend money: rent/mortgage, utilities, automobiles, food, travel, all that stuff.

2) Examine your flexible expenses and look for ways to save. You might start shopping at a food co-op or buy clothes only on sale or at factory outlet stores. On paper, your budget can help you reassign where you want the money to go. For example, if you find you'd really like more money allocated to your family's vacation category, you might decide to cut down on entertainment expenses.

3) Set a savings goal. Based on your budget, decide how much you can afford to set aside each month, however small – and stick to it. When the going gets tough, just keep reminding yourself that you're setting aside the money for your own home or the kids' tuition.

✘ *Dry cleaning:* Before dry cleaning anything valuable, remove fancy buttons, ornate trim, etc. This not only saves you the heartache of a ruined heirloom, but you won't have to deal with the headache of getting the dry cleaner to make good on it.

✘ *Storing safely:* Don't use blue tissue paper when storing anything. The dye can rub off and ruin the items.

✘ *Plastic:* Use clear plastic bags for seasonal, short-term storage of clothing. Even a resealable plastic sandwich bag might do for small things, like gloves. But for bulkier items, like winter coats, suits and dresses, a garment bag from a good notions store is a must.

✘ *Long-term storage:* Make a container out of polyethylene plastic sheeting. Cut two sheets of plastic a bit larger than the size of the item to be stored, slip it in, squeeze out the air and tape all outside edges shut. Throw in a silica-gel packet to keep out moisture.

✘ *Hired household helpers:* In each room to be worked on, post a checklist on an index card with specific cleaning instructions for that room. Tape it to the light switch.

✘ *Buy in bulk:* Transfer some of the bulk product into a leftover regular-size container of the same product so it's easy to lift when you use it.

✘ *Broom-saver:* Soak a new broom in salt water to keep it lasting longer.

✘ *Screens:* To keep screens from rusting, brush both sides with a little kerosene, then wipe them clean with a dry cloth.

✘ *Conserve cashmere:* Prevent damage to this pricey wool by carrying a hand-held purse rather than a shoulder bag. The strap's friction can rub the fabric bare.

✘ *Grocery price list:* Keep your own little black book of prices. Once you get to know the rock-bottom prices of items you usually buy, you'll know what prices are best for picking up some extras.

✘ *Price reductions:* Don't be fooled by reductions in price from "list." Hardly any major item sells for list price. If there's something you want, check out comparables and keep a list. Then you'll know a real sale when it occurs.

✘ *Consumer magazines:* Whenever you're in the market for a major purchase, check out the consumers' magazines. You'll get the low-down on any item so you can make a better buying decision.

✘ *Ironing:* Even if a garment is only slightly stained, don't press it. Heat from the iron will further set the stain. Dry-clean or wash the item first.

✘ *Deodorant:* Chemicals in deodorants can cause fibers to weaken. Wait until your deodorant has completely dried before dressing.

✘ *Footwear:* Buy the best shoes that you can afford. A really good pair of shoes can be resoled over and over and will last for years.

✘ *Shoe trees:* Use shoe trees and cardboard tubes for your boots. They prolong the life of your footwear and protect their shape.

✘ *Auto mechanic:* Comparison shop for a reliable auto mechanic. Waiting until your car breaks down to find one is too late and could be very costly.

✘ *Loose change:* Keep a supply of empty coin rolls handy for sorting all that extra change. When a financial emergency crops up, you can turn these coins into hard cash in a flash.

✘ *Safe-deposit list:* Keep a list at home of what you've got stashed in your safety deposit box.

✘ *Safe-deposit box:* Check with your insurance company to be sure that the contents of your safe-deposit box are covered under your homeowner's policy.

✘ *Protect eyeglasses:* When you're painting, cover each lens with a small patch of clear plastic wrap. When the painting's done, those ghastly globs of paint will just peel away with the plastic.

✘ *Repair list:* Keep a list of everything that needs repair. Add to it as new things crop up. You'll find it's easier – and cheaper – to fix a bunch of things at once.

✘ *Books:* On the inside of all your books, paste a name sticker or use a rubber stamp to identify them as yours.

✘ *Economical packing materials:* When you move, use towels, washcloths and other small linens to pack breakables. Popcorn (the real kind) also makes a terrific, inexpensive, environmentally safe alternative. And you can snack when you unpack!

✘ *Tomato paste:* When you open a can of tomato paste and need just 1 Tbs for a recipe, spoon out the remainder in Tbs-sized portions, place on waxed paper and freeze. Then just peel off one at a time when needed.

✘ *Leftover tomato juice:* Pour the juice from canned tomatoes into ice cube trays and, when frozen, store the batch of tomato cubes in plastic freezer bags. It makes a great savory addition for cooking.

Details, Details, Details
Planning Ahead

✐ **Hanging wallpaper:** Snip a piece off the roll (at a section that has the cleaning info on the back) and file it with your household records. Then, when a spot gets grimy or damaged, you can clean it safely.

✐ **Space for wallpapering:** To improvise a table, use a slab door from any room in the house. The paste spills will wash off easily. For even more space, lay a 4-by-8 sheet of plywood across a bed.

✐ **Replacing hangings:** Stick a toothpick into each nail hole before applying the paper. As you press the paper to the wall, the toothpicks stab through, letting you know where each hole is.

✐ **Water-using appliances:** Whenever installing a water softener, automatic icemaker, etc., also add a valve in the water line – near the appliance. Then you can easily turn off the water in an emergency.

✐ **Chopping nuts:** Cull out the perfect ones first and freeze them. Next time you need some, just scoop them from the freezer.

✐ **Sensible shopping:** Menu plan and shop just once a

week. This way you know exactly what you have, what you need, and can stretch menu items so there's no waste.

Home for sale: If you plan to sell your home, paint the front door, basement walls and the rooms that need it (in neutral colors); wash windows, baseboards and sills; mow and fertilize the lawn...and get rid of the trash.

Perm preview: Set your hair in very small hot rollers and spray heavily with extra-holding hair spray. If you don't like it, shampoo out. If you do, go for the real thing.

Dry cleaners: Test-run a new dry cleaning establishment with your less valuable things to see how they're handled. Then select the best place.

Selecting a pet: Think carefully before selecting a pet. A labrador needs to walk as much as eight miles a day, for example, while miniatures need only half a mile.

Kitchen fire safety: When heating fat in a frying pan, keep a lid or cookie sheet near the stove. In a flash, you can grab it to block air from the pan. They're better than a fire extinguisher, which could splatter the fat and fan the fire.

Cook's clothing: Never wear loose, long-sleeved clothing while standing over a hot stove – and absolutely, positively, never wear a tie.

Toxic materials: If you must answer the doorbell or telephone while working with toxic household polishes or cleaners, tote them with you when you do. Left unattended, they could cause severe accidents to pets or children.

✐ **Travel wardrobe:** Plan wardrobe for a family trip using a commercial cloakroom coat rack. Keep it in the garage and hang garments you want as you think of them.

✐ **Trip planning:** Before traveling, set up files for each place you plan to visit. Collect guidebooks, maps and transportation information and write ahead for tickets to upcoming special events.

✐ **Closing-up checklist:** Enter a checklist of standard locking-up procedures in your computer and print it out or just leave it on paper – before leaving on a trip. Remind yourself to turn off the A/C, close windows, set timers, etc. For last-minute checks, keep the list with your suitcases or post it on the inside of the front door.

✐ **Efficient packing:** Try packing just the right amounts you think you'll need of such disposable items as shampoo, body lotion, soap and toothpaste. That way, you'll use them up, leaving room to bring home those special new trinkets.

✐ **Gasoline:** Put an empty gasoline can in your trunk – it could come in handy if you're ever stranded. NEVER keep a full can of gasoline in your car trunk, however. It could explode if you were rear-ended.

✐ **Trunk essentials:** Keep the following in your trunk: spare tire, jack, lug wrench, flashlight, jumper cables, emergency flares, spare fuses, fan belt, duct tape, adjustable wrench, screwdriver set, work gloves, utility knife, siphon hose, a quart of oil and, depending on where you live, a snow scraper and lock de-icer.

✐ **Boat trailer:** Keep a spare tire on board for your boat trailer.

✐ **Boat key:** Secure your boat key to a cork. If it falls in the water, at least it'll float.

✐ ***Moving survival:*** In a separate bag, pack toilet paper, soap, towels, cleansing powder, paper towels, instant coffee, cups, spoons, light bulbs, can opener and first-aid kit. Take enough clothing to last several days – you never know when the van will arrive.

✐ ***Storing collections:*** If you collect CDs, books, photos, stamps, whatever, choose a system that allows for expansion. The rule of thumb is to plan for twice the capacity you now need.

✐ ***Plan repairs:*** Keep a list throughout the year of the jobs that need to be done. It also helps you make sure you have all the necessary materials on hand that you'll need when you start.

✐ ***Finish the job:*** Before beginning a repair job, make sure you've got all the materials you need.

✐ ***Set repair goals:*** With notebook in hand, survey your house room by room and decide what you want to change or repair. Establish a short-, medium- and long-term goal for each room. Focus on one room at a time and tackle the short-term jobs first.

✐ ***Patio planning:*** First stake it off; then set your barbecue grill and furniture in place. Finally, have a dry-run with as many friends as you think you'll ever entertain outdoors.

✐ ***Plan your day:*** You'll accomplish much more if you prepare a daily to-do list.

✐ ***Prioritize:*** List and number your chores in their order of importance. Always do first things first rather than leaving the hard stuff for the end of the day, when you're frazzled and tired.

✐ ***Avoid oversleeping:*** Set two alarm clocks – one electric and one battery-operated (in case of a power failure). Set them five or 10 minutes apart and place them across the room so you'll have to get out of bed – *twice* – to turn them off.

🖉 **Painting basement steps:** Paint every other step. When those have dried, finish the job.

🖉 **Selecting paint colors:** First invest in a pint of the paint and apply it to a small section of your wall. It can be easily covered over if it's not quite right.

🖉 **Paint test:** Paint a piece of white poster board with the color you've selected, and tape it to the wall to preview what the color will look like.

🖉 **Buy plentiful paint:** Buy enough cans of paint to complete the entire job, and make sure they're from the same batch number.

🖉 **Raw eggs:** If you're toting them to a campout, bury them in a bag of flour or a can of coffee to protect them.

🖉 **Camping matches:** To be sure they light when you need them, dip the heads in linseed oil before setting out on your trip. When dry, they'll be waterproof. Or, wrap untreated matches tightly in aluminum foil.

🖉 **Appointment calendar:** Use your calendar to help remind you to prepare for certain appointments. If, for example, you need to call your accountant about taxes in February, jot down a note on an earlier date to cue you to prepare.

🖉 **Planning big purchases:** List five big items you'd like to buy within the next six months. Keep the list with you and, as you're out and about, keep track of the prices you see in various stores.

...And Then Some...

✸ **Start now:** No matter what the task is, do it now rather than later.

✸ **Get enough sleep:** To function at top form, figure out how long it takes you to fall asleep. Subtract that from the time you normally hit the sack and that's your goal bedtime.

✸ **Reduce visual clutter:** Take a long, hard look at everything in your house within sight. If you don't like something anymore, or have no use for it, toss it. If you just can't bear to dump it, consider storing it.

✸ **Banish clutter:** If you can't decide whether or not to part with something, ask yourself how difficult or expensive it would be to replace it if you had to. Remember, you are in control of your stuff, not the other way around.

✸ **Toss it:** If you haven't touched your craft or hobby supplies for ages (and know in your heart you'll never finish that half-knitted sweater), let them go.

✸ **Take time out:** If you're just too, too hassled, and all else fails, slow down your pace for a minute.

✸ **Set mini-goals:** Divide any project into bite-size pieces and move one step at a time on each before going on to another. Establishing small goals makes it easier to chart your progress.

✹ ***First things first:*** Give less attention and effort to less important matters. Only you know what those are.

✹ ***Learn to delegate:*** When you delegate, make sure you keep the jobs you really enjoy for yourself.

✹ ***Schedule starting time:*** Do it even if it's a month from now. And start anywhere – even at the middle. Don't expect inspiration to make the decision for you.

HOW TO PACK A SUITCASE

- Pack heavy items such as shoes, hair dryer and toiletries in the bottom (the side opposite the handle.)
- Roll up all the stuff that's wrinkle-resistant, like jeans, sweatshirts, sweaters and bathrobes. Place these on the bottom alongside the heavy things you packed first.
- Now add suits, slacks and dresses, laying in the heaviest items first. Let the ends of each garment hang over the edge until you put the next layer in place.
- As you fill the case – one garment at a time, one on top of the other – fold the ends of the previous garment over the edge of the next. This reduces creases and allows you to fill the suitcase evenly.
- At each step in the process, smooth any wrinkles from the clothing.
- Finally, lay in blouses and shirts, following the same procedure. Or, if possible, slip each blouse individually into those plastic bags that come with your dry cleaning. The bags trap the air and keep the contents wrinkle-free.

✹ *Motivate yourself:* Throw a party so you'll have a reason to clean that patio furniture.

✹ *Be flexible:* If your plans to do something suddenly change, work on some other project instead.

✹ *Estimate realistically:* Learn to estimate just how much time a project really takes. That way you can set aside the appropriate amount of time – and you won't feel guilty spending too much time on something.

✹ *Don't overdo:* Don't buy so many organizing items that you'll need an organizer to organize the organizers.

✹ *You're not superwoman:* Recognize that the standards you set may be too high or unrealistic. Try not to demand so much of yourself.

✹ *Mom's shortcuts:* To feel great about how you look – and still trim down the time it takes to get ready for work – get a wash-and-wear haircut.

✹ *Telling time:* If you're s-o-o-o-o organized that you insist on wearing a watch even while you paint, put clear plastic wrap over the watch face to protect it.

✹ *Garage sale signs:* If you're not permitted to put up signs in your neighborhood, use washable white paint to scrawl the words "Garage Sale" on the side of your car and park it on the street near your driveway.

✹ *Mower cord protection:* To make sure you don't run over the cord of your electric lawn mower while you work, make it highly visible. Wrap the cord with colorful tape in a spiral pattern.

✹ *Extra photo film:* Keep some on hand. As soon as you finish one roll, take it out and load a new one. Label the canister you remove with the date and subject.

GLOBE DIGEST SERIES

If you enjoyed this book... then you'll want to order these other Globe Digest favorites!

- 123 650 Home Remedies
- 207 Why Women Get the Blues
- 212 Great Men & Women of the Bible
- 222 "I Wish I'd Thought Of That!"
- 306 How To Read Palms
- 404 Why Do Cats Sulk?
- 410 Christmas Fun for Kids
- 411 The Healing Power of Garlic

Mail to: Globe Digest Series, P.O. Box 114, Rouses Point, NY 12979-0114

Please check the desired title numbers below:
- ☐ 123 ☐ 207
- ☐ 212 ☐ 222
- ☐ 306 ☐ 404
- ☐ 410 ☐ 411

YES! Please send me the titles I've checked – each at $2.29 ($2.79 in Canada) plus .95¢ each for shipping & handling. With my order of 3 or more titles, I save all shipping & handling costs.

D38

Name_____
PLEASE PRINT

Address_____

City_____ St_____ Zip_____

PLEASE COMPLETE

U.S. Only: I enclose total of $3.24 for each of ____titles equaling $_____
(if ordering 3 or more titles, enclose only $2.29 for each)

Canadian Only: I enclose total of $3.74 for each of ____titles equaling $_____
(if ordering 3 or more titles, enclose only $2.79 for each)

Please allow 4 to 8 weeks for your order to arrive.